Reading rights for boys

Reading rights for boys

Sex role in language experience

DAVID E. AUSTIN
VELMA B. CLARK
GLADYS W. FITCHETT

ALL CONSULTANTS TO
THE MERCED COUNTY, CALIFORNIA, SCHOOLS

APPLETON-CENTURY-CROFTS
EDUCATIONAL DIVISION
MEREDITH CORPORATION

New York

CONTENTS

Foreword

Education that is active, exploratory, problem-solving, adventurous, and aggressive has been talked about for a long time, but little has been done. A current interest in providing equality of educational opportunity for boys and girls has revived the talk and hopefully will result in action.

Reading Rights for Boys is written by three teachers who, for a long time, have had deep concerns for the unreasonable percentage of boys who fail in reading in elementary grades. They have worked with hundreds of teachers, both male and female, to identify some of the problems of boys in the school setting. They have worked diligently to discover solutions which give boys an even break with girls, especially in beginning reading. The authors are aware that what we know today about boy-school conflict and failure, especially in reading and language development, is primitive. They do not propose final answers. Rather, they share the results of their study, experience, and exploration on the subject. They explain the philosophical and psychological bases for their proposals and then provide a wealth of suggestions for implementing a school program with objectives for giving boys an equal chance with girls in academic pursuits.

Very early in the book the authors make clear that they do not view the problem as one of having mostly women teachers in American elementary schools. Rather, they point out that school is too much a woman's world governed by women's rules and standards. The school code is that of propriety, obedience, decorum, cleanliness, silence, physical, and too often, mental passivity. Such a code brews trouble with boys and for boys—trouble which is unnecessary and undesirable.

Evidence of the trouble is reported frequently in low achievement scores. These scores cluster in the area of "reading achievement" to such an extent that the problem is often viewed as a "reading problem."

Unfortunately, the problem has much deeper and vital roots than that of "reading failure." The masculine virtues are usually diametrically opposite to those viewed as desirable in the typical American elementary school. The boys of our society who are labeled "little men" are aggressive—not passive. They are active and in motion rather than still. They are independent more than they are obedient. They speak out rather than keep quiet. Many of them love conflict, struggle, and a good fight rather than perpetual peace. The female code under which they operate at school is one of making as much effort as possible in *studies* of what is known already—what is printed in books. The male code of young boys is one of making the least possible effort in "book studies." They are forever satisfying their need to know by observing, listening, exploring, tearing up, putting together, trying out, and in general "just messing around."

The authors of *Reading Rights for Boys* detail classroom organization in which it is feasible for boys to pursue their masculine style and achieve, at the same time, the basic skills necessary for successful communication through listening, speaking, writing, and reading. The personal experiences of the authors, as well as observations of other teachers, assures that the suggestions are practical.

The school woes of boys are not pictured as being ended when the school's style is adjusted to promote exploration, problem-solving, and self-expression activities. A companion woe which is pursued is that of feminine, frilly content, especially in reading and language development materials. Until recently, publishing efforts have provided little reading material with male interests as a central concern. Very few classroom teachers have been furnished with these materials as basic ones for instruction. The choice open to them as reading teachers is a "female" or "neuter" orientation when selecting beginning reading materials. By the time the male failures are old enough to read well-developed stories with male interests in the intermediate grades, they can't! This dilemma has resulted in a rash of special reading teachers, remedial classes, federally financed study projects, research in methods of teaching beginning reading, and the application of electronics to existing or "alike" reading content.

The general unwillingness of parents and educators to accept the excessive number of reading failures among boys as inevitable has invited the production of many materials which claim to possess quick and easy cures—"pure" phonics approaches, learn to read while you sleep, teach your baby to read, apply the science of linguistic scholars, read by color, concoct a new alphabet, or give children candy when they "unlock new words." None of these sure cures is suggested as a solution in *Reading Rights for Boys*. The authors avoid these and get to fundamental problems of

> *valuing* the thinking of boys and girls, regardless of how limited;
>
> *accepting* the real language of boys and girls, regardless of how divergent from the standard English used in textbooks;
>
> *encouraging* boys and girls to express their thinking in many forms—talking, painting, modeling, acting, constructing, dictating, writing;
>
> *representing* the thinking of individuals in written form by taking dictation, thus assuring a measure of success at all times and at all stages of language development;
>
> *reconstructing* (reading) the written material which reflects the thinking of boys and girls in the classroom—publishing newspapers, magazines, class books, individual books;
>
> *influencing* the thinking of boys and girls through the use of multiple resources—books, films, recordings, study prints, study trips, television, radio—so that their talking, listening, writing, and reading will mature in accordance with their inner drives, ideals, and personal goals.

The mounting evidence of the disproportionate number of boys who are disabled readers, maladjusted, low achievers, delinquent, inattentive and rebellious reinforces and undergirds the urgent need for educational reform in the direction of equal opportunity for boys and girls. This evidence as presented in *Reading Rights for Boys* elicits many questions which remain unanswered at the end of the book. At the same time, the specific suggestions for beginning solutions are adequate for any teacher or administrator who is vitally concerned with the problem.

The three authors, one male and two female, feel sure that whatever improvements are made in the educational climate, methods of instruction, and school materials for the sake of boys will also profit girls.

Roach Van Allen
Professor of Education
University of Arizona
Tucson, Arizona

chapter one

Philosophical distortions and their implications in instruction

There is a fundamental need to examine the discriminating character of the American school as a learning environment for boys. However disturbing this premise may be, mounting evidence indicates clearly that such discrimination exists with almost universal frequency in the classrooms of the nation's schools.

There is little doubt that the character of American education is feminine, either by design or as a comfortable acceptance unintentionally adopted by the teachers and administrators developing the structure of the program. Standards of conduct, restricted environments for learning, the majority members of the instructional staff, academic and social expectations, and the physical setting for the school are all substantially feminine, with little regard for the male culture presented within the societal structure outside of the schools.

A hurried examination of the first false measure of success in the schools will give the reader something of a foundation for an initial insight into the non-male form of the classroom. The standards of conduct attributed to terms such as "quiet," "orderly," and "obedient" may well be used to describe a well-functioning American classroom. Indeed, these are traditional guideposts for administrative assessments of the effectiveness of classroom instruction.

However frequently educators use such terms in evaluations of "good" teaching, they are directly contrary to the societal expectations of boys. Such restrictions must have detrimental effects upon the boys assigned to these classrooms.

Societal expectations

In a list of terms ascribed to boys functioning in accord with societal expectations, the terms below are normally found:

active	imaginative
adventuresome	robust
brave	outspoken
curious	disheveled
dirty	rough

To pursue this type of examination further is unnecessary. It can be said, that boys who lack these characteristics do not fit the societal form. For a girl to possess any of these traits would be to place her in the unpopular position of being a tomboy. These qualities are expected of boys outside the classroom, yet in school such terms are used to describe boys not fitting the proper academic mold.

To be quite fair, it is necessary to make a comparable list of terms descriptive of society's expectations for girls. It would frequently include those presented below:

neat	artistic
quiet	studious
mannerly	sensitive
pretty	obedient
clean	gentle

It is obvious which of the two lists more aptly describes the type of child readily accepted in the classroom. Indeed, given two children, one with the characteristics ascribed to boys and one with those ascribed to girls, the traditional educator would be nearly ready to predict the ultimate success or failure pattern for each of these children through their school careers. All of this assumes, of course, that the child with the traits ascribed to boys would be unwilling to adopt the patterns insuring success in school: those characteristics patterned for girls. Thus boys are forced to function in accord with dual standards: one for in school and one for out of school.

Alan Cline, a journalist and education writer for the *San Francisco Examiner* and *Chronicle*[1] poses some disturbing questions for educators. Each of these noted below could well form the basis for further examination among teachers. Mr. Cline asks,

Do girls really do better in the early grades, or do teachers just think (that) they do?

. . . are girls surrendering their own desires and ability to be aggressive and think unconventionally because they know they have a conforming role to play?

Mr. Cline partially answers the questions when he goes on to say:

It is possible American society is depriving itself of potential male artists and potential female scientists because neither sex was encouraged to follow these paths.

If the reader can, through such a cursory review of the status of boys, formulate questions about the non-male structure of our public schools, then it would seem appropriate to examine the feminine character of these schools.

The learning experiences of boys and girls during the preschool years overlap in numerous respects, but are unique to each sex in others. Many of these differences are cultural dictations, but they exist in the learning experiences for young children nevertheless. The very patterns of children's dress take on forms that separate the boys from the girls. Frilly dresses not only look nice on little girls, but they reflect the type of conduct expected of them. Blue jeans and denim jackets for boys tell them that they are expected to be robust and get dirty in the course of their activities. Masculine conversations between boys and their mothers or fathers fully establish "out-spoken" patterns during these most formative preschool years. This training is misleading for boys, however, and they are due to have disturbing experiences when being first enrolled in school. These preschool habits are not acceptable in the eyes of the educational system. Adventure-

[1] Alan Cline, "School Practices Favor Girls, Educators Find," *San Francisco Examiner and Chronicle*, (December 8, 1966).

some exploration as a carefully developed trait among boys, or girls for that matter, is inconsistent with the formal structure of the in-school learning environment.

Boys, having developed the features of "normal boys," are confronted with a serious choice relative to their performance upon entering school. The young male must either forego his prior training and adopt the obedient patterns of the school setting or he must reject the school program.

Prescott Lecky asks a question relative to the problem confronting boys and then provides a partial answer.[2] He asks,
Why (are) boys slower than girls in learning to read?
The behavior of the child in the classroom must also be understood in terms of the standards he is trying to maintain. Let us take, for example, the well known fact that boys on the average are slower than girls in learning to read. Educational textbooks usually explain this by saying that girls have more native ability in respect to reading than boys. In terms of self-consistency, however, the explanation is that to most boys the reading material in elementary readers seems infantile and effeminate.

Lecky's statement demonstrates that boys are stronger in "self-consistency" traits and that they would rather accept the penalties of being less acceptable in the eyes of educators than surrender to the feminine structure of the school and its curriculum.

Agreement with the precepts presented by Lecky would force educators to conclude that boys make a choice between acceptance of school form or retention of male self-consistency at the first confrontation with the school program. Indeed, boys and girls make this choice within the first few days of their first year in the classroom. It is undoubtedly disturbing to educators to realize that children are capable of "reading" the intent of the instructional environment so quickly. Therefore, it is much more comfortable for teachers to accept traditional explanations for the early separation of performance levels between boys and girls.

[2] Prescott Lecky, *Self-Consistency: A Theory of Personality*, (New York, The Shoe String Press, Inc., 1961), p. 250.

Early verbal foundations

Some educators explain the differences between the performance levels of boys and girls as the product of native characteristics. That is, girls have a verbal character and therefore perform better and earlier in school than do the nonverbal boys. Acceptance of this explanation would conclude this study of sex differences without further examination. Such acceptance, however, would exclude the possibility that boys reject the structure of the instructional setting and the curriculum prescribed for them. Further, these conclusions would exclude the findings of much current research relative to performance and sex differences. Loretta Byers states that there is a need for a language curriculum which is highly flexible and makes allowances for sex differences among students. Byers further describes this need when she says,[3]

. . . content should be assessed for its appeal to boys. Differences in interests of boys and girls in the study suggest that current content (of textbooks) may more often be geared to the major interests of girls than of boys. Boys' interests in outdoor activities such as fishing, vacations and excursions, swimming, horseback riding, and bicycle riding are seldom reflected in first grade readers; nor is there much content dealing with joint activities of father and son.

The exclusion of male interests from language materials provides boys with substantial reasons for rejecting the instructional program. It is possible, though, that other factors are as important in this rejection as the lack of appropriate book interest elements. A combination of active oral experiences must also be considered as a factor in the relative progress of boys in the field of reading and language. The tradition of the national culture must be considered as oral in character. This oral tradition is substantially pronounced during the years prior to the confrontation with the school program.

All experiences prior to the child's enrollment in school are either action oriented with description in the oral form or are imaginative experiences formulated in the spoken language. Even the stories read to the young child by his parents are likely to be translated into

---

[3] Loretta Byers, "Pupils' Interests and the Content of Primary Reading Texts," *The Reading Teacher*, (January 1964), pp. 227–233.

personal experiences and presented in oral interpretation. Each is uniquely personal and relative only to the individual child. Acceptance of these experiences must not be interpreted as acceptance of the printed form of the story presented to the child, but rather as acceptance of the orally translated, personal interpretations made by the child.

Recognition of orally formed environments on a uniquely personal level presents the boy with still another reason for rejecting traditional instructional program materials. For the boy to be grouped with other children of like performance levels and to be presented with stories lacking his particular interest elements and to know that there is a group translation of the story, removes the possibility of having a uniquely personal experience with the printed material. Moreover, to confront the child with the necessity for translating the printed form itself into some meaning rather than translating the experiences of the story—a process contrary to prior experiences—cannot be satisfying to any child, especially to boys.

Research indicates that boys and girls arrive at the first year in school with essentially the same vocabulary capabilities. Ames' study found that ". . . no significant differences were found in the size of basic understanding vocabulary of grade one boys and girls."[4] In effect, boys and girls have equal verbal foundations upon which to build their reading and language understandings. Differences in language development, then, occur *following entry in school* even though the boys and girls are provided with the same materials for learning and subjected to the same methods of instruction. The fault, then, would appear to be inherent within the program and not within the boys themselves.

Pursuing the precept that the program is at fault, a study by Durkin is relevant.[5] Durkin found ". . . that a typical second-grade reading program, as contrasted with a typical first-grade program, is more likely to offer instruction that is appropriately challenging . . . and that boys, more than girls, profit from the challenge." Durkin's study brings us full circle and once again we look at the findings of

[4] Wilbur S. Ames, "The Understanding Vocabulary of First Grade Pupils," *Elementary English*, (January, 1964), pp. 64–68.
[5] Delores Durkin, "The Achievement of Pre-School Readers, Two Longitudinal Studies," *Reading Research Quarterly*, (Summer, 1966), pp. 5–36.

Prescott Lecky relative to "self-consistency."[6] It will be recalled that Lecky determined: "In terms of self-consistency . . . to most boys the reading material in elementary readers seems infantile and effeminate."

This publication is not meant to present an exhaustive search of studies supportive of their contentions that schools fail to provide boys with an appropriate program in reading and language development. Such information is readily available and references are provided in the bibliography at the end of the chapter.

Provisions considerate of reading and language development

Providing for the male interests in a program of reading and language development will require substantive changes in the existing structure. Moreover, it is likely that these changes will be contrary to the form of traditional instruction in this field and, therefore, not easily accomplished within the frame of reference presently accepted by school teachers. Further, in making the desired changes in the curriculum and instructional methods, educators must not shift their positions to the extent that girls' interests are subordinated in the process. One would be well advised to consider, however, that many girls are equally at home in both masculine and in feminine environments.

Educators must, also, use caution in the selection of program elements in order that they do not develop what in fact will be a sexless type of program with respect to the interests and performance differences between boys and girls. It would be quite possible to end up with a program so neutral as to be of no real interest or value to either of the sexes.

Being fully cognizant of the complexities of developing programs which provide for a broad range of interests for both sexes, it is felt that such programs must be open in character. Through this openness, a freedom will be provided for each child to pursue his particular interests and vary them in accord with the pace which he or she may desire. With this basic premise in mind, a program should be

[6] Prescott Lecky, Op. Cit.

developed which places the greatest possible stress upon the child's own language forms and understanding vocabulary.

In subsequent chapters of this book, the reader shall have opportunities to explore a variety of instructional techniques and resources appropriate to the formation of a program considerate of male interests. In the remaining pages of this chapter, however, implications for the classroom program are noted. This notation is not intended to be exhaustive, but rather to include sufficient suggestions to allow for full recognition of the extent of change needed to accommodate boys.

Implications for the instructional program

Each implication presented in the following pages is formed as a question. It would be most presumptuous to assume complete knowledge of the changes needed. Rather, it is intended that through these questions and the comments that follow many directions for needed change will be perceived. A teacher can build programs appropriate to his particular teaching circumstances. It is also intended that each question will serve as a foundation for further study and the formulation of new data and substantially better-based programs in reading and language instruction.

1. *What changes are needed in the selection of instructional materials used in the primary grades in order that provisions may be made for male interests at this level?*

In the precise selection of materials for instruction, especially in the field of reading and language, attention must be given to selections which will stimulate exploration by boys and develop an intense curiosity. With this frame of reference, the selection of non-textbook items would seem most appropriate, inasmuch as traditional texts are restrictive in as many cases as they are stimulating. The organization of what are called "centers of interest" would seem more appropriate. Centers of interest might include the types of materials boys would enjoy: i.e., rocks, simple machines, all manner of flora and fauna, pictures and picture books representative of boys' interests, and other similar materials.

The purpose of the instructional materials selected for use in the classroom is not to provide the total scope of the program of instruction, as would be true in the case of basal reading or language textbooks. Rather, it is intended that the selection of materials be such as to stimulate the kinds of fascinating explorations which would result in a desire among the students to talk about what they have seen and want to ask questions which would formulate the basis for further study. Each of these oral expressions, first recorded on experience charts by the teacher and later by each student in his own written form, provides the foundation for learning to read and write. The primary difference between such forms of printed materials and those found in the traditional basal readers is in the formation of these materials. These materials are developed in strict accord with the expressions of the individual child and in character with his particular interests.

The teacher's task, then, is to structure a *learning laboratory* made up of as many interest centers as is possible.

2. *What specific implications are there for staffing pattern changes, particularly in the primary grades?*

The need for male primary teachers is, of course, the most obvious. The placement of men in the lower elementary grades is not a new concept. The need for men in these lower grades is well substantiated, however old the concept may be and however short the supply of such teachers has been. If qualified male teachers cannot be found for the primary grades, however, it is possible in many districts to get teacher's aides or teacher's assistants for these classrooms. In these instances, men could be selected to serve with a professional teacher and, in this way, form a balanced male and female team.

In those instances in which additional staff cannot be had and in circumstances in which it is not possible to induce men to teach in the primary grades, serious consideration must be given to the selection of teachers with the ability to demonstrate sincere interest in fields similar to those the boys in her class may possess. The need for teachers to be at one minute interested in the robust activities and concerns of boys, and at the next to be able to demonstrate with equal sincerity interest in the unique concerns of girls, cannot be minimized. There is no need for a constant mother figure among teachers in the primary grades.

Lacking all of the above, a school might better utilise the resource personalities of the community, particularly with attention to men. The fathers of the children in the classes, the various city employees such as firemen, policemen, and businessmen, can each serve as male models for the instructional program. The frequency of visits by such persons, however, must be great to have much value. If such visits are too infrequent they will serve to further stress the feminine character of the classroom.

Most fundamental to the adequate staffing of primary grade classrooms, however, is the careful selection of persons cognizant of the varied interests of boys as being different from those of girls. Even with such selections, it will be necessary to provide a continuous in-service education program for the teachers with attention to this most important problem.

3. *What are the implications for changes needed in the disciplinary structure of the classroom?*

Rigid adherence to the structures of traditional classrooms must be recognized as detrimental to the individual growth of all children, but particularly to the growth of boys. As has been noted in this chapter, the orderly standards of a classroom are inconsistent with the action-oriented training and expectations for boys outside school.

Provisions must be made for free exploration and the satisfying of the individual boy's curiosity within the structure of the classroom. Without this, it is possible that the boys will reject the program of the educational system.

It must not be understood from these statements that individual explorations by the children in the classroom should take the form of actions inconsiderate of others. Freedom of movement and individual pacing of studies need not be without regard for the scheduling procedures established by the teacher.

Such freedom of movement for exploration is essential, however, to the appropriate adjustment of the program to the interests of boys—indeed, of all children.

4. *What are the implications for measurement of achievement in a program considerate of male interests?*

If the teacher is to make adjustments in the materials of learning for boys and expect daily performance differences among the boys, then it is logical that identical measures of progress cannot be applied to all children, without regard to sex differences, in the classroom.

Measurements must be established in such a manner as to be thoroughly individualized and not limited by the traditional comparative forms of measurement. The primary concerns should be with respect to the progress in reading and writing skills made by each child in terms of his own abilities and interests. In fact, there is much evidence that present pacing and structured grading of children is based upon a false premise.[7]

[7] Ellis Batten Page, "Teacher Comments and Student Performance: A Seventy-four Classroom Experiment in School Motivation," *Readings in the Social Psychology of Education*, W. W. Charters Jr. and N. L. Gage (eds.), (Boston, Allyn and Bacon, 1963), pp. 219–225.

5. *What are the implications for traditional grouping patterns in a program considerate of male interests?*

> Ability grouping and grouping for achievement in reading and language instruction is a restrictive process inconsistent with the freedom required for individual pacing and exploration. Therefore, it is unlikely that the traditional forms of grouping will be appropriate for the program envisioned. This is not to say that natural interests among the children, particularly the boys, would exclude grouping in a temporary form. Associations of children in the course of explorations of interests certainly will be formed. Also, it would seem likely that the teacher might group some children for specific skills instruction. This grouping would be established, however, in accord with daily lesson preparations and would undoubtedly be highly flexible, with changes in the membership of groups almost daily. Also, it should be recognized that the grouping discussed above would not be for all children. Many children will find it more profitable to function individually and in accord with their specific interests, only being brought into the larger group or a total class group for appreciation of the activities of others or for informative sessions provided by the teacher.

6. *What subtle inferences are in a program considerate of individualized interests?*

> It is necessary for teachers to understand that an individualized, interest-directed program will require delicate scheduling, but not for every minute of the day. For interests to be fully developed and for children to test the depth of their interests, it is necessary that they be given time to simply sit and think. Undue pressure to be "doing something" at all times can, in fact, prevent achievement of the very objectives which a teacher may have for the instructional program.
>
> Further, it must be possible for children, particularly

boys, to realize a number of choices which might determine their study actions. With only subtle direction from the teacher, children must be allowed to vary their choices even subsequent to implementation. It is not inconsistent for boys to test interests by initiating a course of exploration and almost immediately to "skip" to another interest area entirely.

Another factor that can be utilized to a maximum in a program with such inherent freedom as that presented, is the degree to which the talents and interests of peers may play a part in the studies of individual children. Such comments as, "I like your story. Would you like to read it to Bob and see what he thinks of it?" would be quite in order and a well-advised element in the teacher's technique package.

In order that one might pursue the issues presented in this chapter, a number of additional studies are listed below with pertinent references. Each is designed to give further assistance in planning a program that will provide for the unique interests of boys and, also, to be considerate of girls who may have like needs.

REFERENCES

Gates, Arthur I., "Sex Differences in Reading Ability," *Elementary School Journal*, 61: 431–434, May 1961.

Giles, Douglas E., *The Effects of Two Approaches to Reading Instruction Upon the Oral Language Development of First Grade Pupils*, North Texas State University Dissertation Abstracts, 1966.

Hahn, Harry T., *A Study of the Relative Effectiveness of Three Methods of Teaching Reading in Grade One*, Cooperative Research Project No. 2687, U.S. Office of Education, 1965.

Loughlin, Leo J., O'Connor, Henry A., Powell, Marvin, and Parsley, Kenneth M., Jr., "An Investigation of Sex Differences by Intelligence, Subject-Matter Area, Grade and Achievement Level on Three Anxiety Scales," *Journal of Genetic Psychology*, June 1965, pp. 209–215.

Sinks, Naomi, and Powell, Marvin, "Sex and Intelligence Factors in Achievement in Reading in Grades Four through Eight," *Journal of Genetic Psychology*, March 1965, pp. 67–79.

chapter two

The learning process and the perceptual differences between boys and girls

An adequate self-concept is fundamental to success in any field of endeavor. For a child to benefit from the educational process it is essential that he be able to participate in the instructional environment in a personally satisfying manner. This satisfaction can only come through knowing that his participation has an obvious effect on the scope of the environment and the elements to be found within it. In a broad sense, then, the act of learning is the process of shaping and reshaping environments and restructuring one's place in these settings. All of this action must be as a result of personal "manufacturing." Indeed, the more personal the action is, the more successful the experiences in the learning process.

Early perception of environment

Careful consideration must be made of the perceived environments of the individual children in each school setting. Teachers must recognize that children's perceptions of their environments will be largely dependent upon the out-of-school worlds in which they have been performing or expect to be living in rather than upon school experiences. In the instance of younger children, these "perceived environments" will be a curious mixture of "what is now," "what is imagined," and "what has been experienced previously." Temporal harmony is not a factor. Moreover, all environments are perceived in such a manner as will enable the individual child to find his place in the varied settings.

Perceptions of environments will differ among any given group of children. However, in addition to the differences which may exist among children, there are marked perceptual differences between boys and girls. Boys are far more apt to generalize their environments, whereas girls tend to interpret their environments in terms of specific elements. This gives rise to the generally accepted beliefs that girls pay more attention to detail than do boys, therefore they are generally more successful in traditional school programs. The fact is that existing school programs are more consistent with the perceived environments of girls than those of boys.

The short description of a classroom incident given below will illustrate the sharp differences between the perceptions of children and teachers as related to environments:

. . . A teacher, while moving about her classroom during an art activity, stopped by one child's easel to view a painting which the child was preparing. Asking the child what it was that he wanted to portray, the child responded, "It's a picture of God." The surprised teacher said, ". . . but no one known what God looks like." "They will when I am through!" replied the child.

A less confident child might have had this educational experience destroyed by this teacher's limited view of a child's perceived environment. The need is for the teacher to arrange environments in which children can find themselves and in which they can interact with substantial freedom.

Developing classroom environment

Accepting as a working premise, then, the need for the educational setting to become a personal laboratory for each child, certain changes must be effected in the existing structures. Fundamental to the changes needed is the development of a highly flexible environment which can be individually adjusted and "personalized." Predetermined programs of instruction, with their limiting factors, are inconsistent with the concepts of learning laboratories established in this chapter.

Predetermined programs of instruction seldom demonstrate the flexibility requisite for personalizing, which is so important to the child finding his place in the educational system. Such programs assume certain needs and interests on the part of children and, while these programs may be sometimes correct, it can be substantiated that preconceived instructional programs will most certainly not be right for many children.

Further analysis of the working premise established for this chapter will provide insight into the frame of reference being used in this writing. For a school program to be organized in terms of a learning laboratory, it is necessary that each of the characteristics presented below be carefully considered.

a. *Instructional programs* must be highly flexible and reflective of the individual children's expressions of interest and need.

b. *Staffing patterns* should be in terms of teachers and paraprofessionals who recognize that their roles can only be interpreted in the light of learning facilitators or catalysts and not in the traditional sense as directors of learning.

c. *Physical settings* must be highly stimulating with maximum allowances for adjustment to the expressed interests of the students in the classroom. Equipment and learning centers can only be organized around the needs of the children and in terms of their particular interests. "Bookish" structures are quite out of order in the proper physical environments.

d. *Subject matter*, as presented in basic courses of study, must be interpreted as a vehicle for learning and not as a learning end in itself. In this frame of reference, the subjects presented are not for the purpose of developing immediately applied skills, as has been the case of the traditional program, but rather for exploratory experiences which will broaden and enrich the learning laboratories for children.

e.   *Scheduling and grade level pacing* will be flexibly adjusted to the individual child's degree of interest in particular learnings and will not follow traditional period divisions and promotion practices.

f.   *Assessment of achievement and grading* will be adjusted to the individual child and be organized in accord with his own progress. To be effective, the assessment practices must be reflections of the child's own determinations with respect to his degree of success in interaction with his real and conceptualized environments. External assessments must be recognized as having little real value.

The learning processes should be accepted in the light of personal forms with individuality and uniqueness equal to the varied forms represented by the members of the class. Learning is self-directed and successful to the degree of the child's interaction with his learning laboratory. The actions of the teacher and the utilization of materials in the classroom only have meaning to the extent that the pupil wishes and is able to participate in the use of each.

Acceptance of the learning processes as a personal matter requires also the acceptance of the individualization of learning opportunities. Each learning opportunity must have relevance to the particular child and his interests, needs, and motivating factors. Only in this way can a program be established that will have meaning for each child. Further, only in this way can the provisions for male differences be included in the programs of learning.

It is logical to assume, then, that to establish learning laboratories for each child in accord with his particular needs, the teacher must develop rapport with each student to the highest possible degree. The ability of the teacher to establish the form of rapport which allows the student to fully utilize his facilitating talents will have much to do with the success of the learning process. Individual students will include or exclude the teacher in the learning laboratory in accord with his ability to develop this desired rapport. Learning "in spite of the teacher" is the result of a teacher's inability to develop fully this working relationship. Teachers, then, must be fully cognizant of male interests and the varied roles the teacher must play with individual children—each role with equal sincerity.

Through personal studies and interviews with individual students, the teacher will begin to recognize the variations which exist between the individual child's perceptions of the educational system and the setting in which he is working. Moreover, as the teacher progresses through the individual interviews with each child, she will begin to recognize the substantially different interests and perceptions which exist among the boys as opposed to those of the girls.

A chronological determination of the steps which the teacher must use to individualize the instructional programs will proceed from the process of building teacher-pupil rapport to the process of establishing an environment which will reflect the child's expressions of interest. Recognition will be made of the varied vehicles for learning which must be included in the learning laboratories of individual students. The processes of learning to read for one child may come through a consuming interest in snakes, for another through imaginary adventures. Provisions must be made for as many of these vehicles as are represented by the particular interests of each child in the classroom. The inclusion of these vehicles will call for a substantially different format for the presentation of aids to learning. Some vehicles must use books, as is traditional; some may require learning centers in which printed materials are not evident.

Provisions for individualizing learning laboratories can be developed to the extent that each child will participate actively with his particular learning vehicle. Through this process of interaction, desire to communicate with others his feelings and discoveries will provide the basis for language development and the acquisition of the skills of learning to read, write, and speak. Assessments of the effectiveness of these adjustments to the peculiar interests of each child can then be measured in terms of the desire of each pupil to want to communicate with others.

Teachers need to realize that interaction with one's environment may be in many forms. Some children appear to function best in a process of *touch-and-learn:* the process made famous by Fernald.[1] Others may interact with their environment through a combination of *adjustments in elements.* Through the movement of parts and the crea-

[1] Grace M. Fernald, *Remedial Techniques In Basic School Subjects,* (New York, McGraw Hill, 1943).

tion of new settings for the unit of study, the student may gain the insights he desires. Placing elements in order with respect to size, shape, or some other characteristic may give meaning to some children. Still other pupils may learn through a process of deutero learning, for example, a process of quiet observation in which no overt action is taken by the student. In this process, the teacher must be prepared for the student reaction in which there appears to be no action on the part of the child: a process of just sitting and thinking. Unfortunately, traditional methods of measurement of the learning process on a daily basis have made very little provision for "just sitting and thinking."

The formulation of the learning setting must focus first upon the learner, then, and not upon the traditional structures, the teachers, the textbooks to be used, or the physical setting. The learner's perceptions of the needs which he has in the light of the environment which he perceives determine the course of action for the educational structure. Children, living in a sprawling urban slum with all the rats and problems of poverty, must not perceive as very real the need to know the type of clothing worn by Pilgrims in early American history. It is also doubtful that these children will find themselves in the setting of the middle class community represented by the traditional basal reading textbooks.

Self-perception and the learning process

The student's progress is determined by his ability to interact with his environment. If the pupil cannot find himself in the setting prepared by educators, then it is unlikely that he will succeed in the learning processes. Further, each child must reconcile his participation in accord with his perceptions of himself.

Participation is determined, in a large measure, by the degree to which the child, particularly the boy, can remain consistent with his self-concept. This self-concept, it will be remembered, is a product of personal development and interpretations of self in the light of societal expectations.[2]

[2] Prescott Lecky, *Self-Consistency: A Theory of Personality*, (New York, The Shoe String Press, Inc., 1961) pp. 6–7.

Programs of instruction which force the abridging of the self-concept cannot help damage the learning process for the individual. However, an atmosphere conducive to learning which capitalizes upon the child's image or perceptions of himself will produce an almost unlimited force for learning.

Keeping in mind, then, that learning is a personalized process and that each child perceives his environment in a different manner from the perceptions of another child, and further, that boys view their world of participation differently from girls, it becomes obvious that group determinations for instruction are most likely to be built upon false foundations. Damage to learning, rather than assistance, will come from programs forcing boys to perform "experiences" which they perceive as feminine. Perhaps the reverse is also true, although there is less evidence to support the damaging results from girls performing masculine tasks.

The teacher also needs to understand that when learning is self-directed, trial-and-error methods are less threatening. If the child attempts a task of his own volition, but with the support of the teacher and the environment, and fails, it is possible for him to assess such failure intelligently. He can review his course of action and determine what he should have done differently. All of this he can accomplish without damage to his self-concept. However, if the teacher assigns a task and the child fails to accomplish it with real success, the failure is assessed by the child in terms of failure in relationships with another person. This is substantially more damaging and reflects sharply upon the child's feelings of adequacy.

Sometimes teachers, in their sincere desire to insure against failures, will break the unit of study into such small parts as to make the learning meaningless and, at the very best, monotonous. Having broken the study units into small parts, the teacher may well have insulted the boy's image of his learning abilities. Moreover, when the monotony of such instruction—in which the child can project activities well in advance of performance—fails, the threat to the student's perceptions of himself is markedly more severe. It is important for the teacher to understand that it is not possible for an "outsider" to make this type of determination for children. Each student must prescribe his own "units" of learning and pace himself in accord with his perceptions of what he can do successfully.

In terms of language development, then, it is necessary for the teacher to view language as a form of personality development. The language forms which the child possesses upon arrival in a school classroom reflect his personality development in the period prior to school. The degree to which these differences in personality and langauge forms are maintained and strengthened during the years in school is indicative of the successful individualization of the learning processes. Respect for these differences is as essential to human relationships and the development of the unique personalities as respect for physical differences. The teacher would not think of attempting to alter skin coloring. Neither should she attempt to force an externally perceived language pattern upon a child.

It is readily recognized that among adult authors, the very ability to develop unique techniques of expression is the skill that is respected. Dr. Seuss is highly regarded, not because of the content of his writing, but more because of the unique patterns of expression which he employs. This type of inventiveness makes the reading more delightful, particularly to boys. And this is as it should be with children in the classroom.

To provide satisfactorily for the precepts presented in the foregoing remarks, certain implications for change in the present mode of instruction will become apparent. The implications provided in the remaining pages of this chapter are not all-inclusive, but, rather, are suggestive of the changes needed.

Implications for the instructional program

1. *Assuming the fundamental truths presented in this chapter, what considerations must be given to insure children of adequate self-concepts while at the same time maintaining the disciplinary standards essential in the classroom?*

> Teachers must understand fully that when placing children in truly exciting learning environments there is little need for external measures to "control" the behavior of the members of the class. Children who feel good about themselves are seldom problems in the classroom. However, it is also important for teachers to understand that learning takes place only in environ-

ments which students perceive to be essentially free of constraints. This understanding should not be difficult for educators to accept inasmuch as such an understanding is basic to the American way of life. Were it not for the great degrees of freedom which exist in our nation, the enormous strides in social and scientific progress could not have been made. There will be, of course, more activity and more noise in the type of learning environment which allows for freedom of direction and individual exploration so important to boys. Also, there will be substantially more progress by the students and greater satisfactions for the teacher.

2. *Is it implied that in this type of program there will be no grouping of children for learning purposes?*

Although this question will be answered in more detail later, it can be understood that the question might arise at this time. Grouping of children is, of course, only of value when such grouping is for specific purposes. Common needs will be identified for several students in the class. These needs may include such factors as weaknesses in phonics, spelling, sentence structure, or any of the usually identified needs of students in a language program. The difference in grouping in the type of program suggested here lies in the area of prior student identification of these same needs. In effect, the teacher is not saying, "On Thursday of this week, I will ask all of the students in this group to work with me on long and short vowel sounds." Rather, students will be expressing their needs in their writing and the grouping will be organized after the discovery of these weaknesses. Moreover, the grouping of students will be done to place those students with common needs in a temporary group for the necessary instruction. Seldom will there be a necessity for the same children to be grouped together. Particularly important, however, is the recognition that such grouping is not programmed in advance by the teacher.

3. In this type of program, will the students be completely free to pursue their individual interests without regard for broad programs developed by the teacher?

> From the student's standpoint, it is important that such an understanding be perceived as true. However, teachers will recognize fully the need to establish goals with the children, particularly in terms of desired behaviors. The attainment of such goals will require careful guidance by the teacher in forms of subtle stimulation and direction. Also, achievement of these goals must be accepted through a variety of courses of action by the students. The ability of the teacher to develop stimulating learning environments which will be highly interesting to individual pupils and yet carefully formed to be consistent with the goals desired must be viewed as essential to successful teaching. Precise programming of instruction will, however, not be a part of the learning environment.

4. If teachers and para-professionals are to serve as "learning facilitators," what kinds of understandings and backgrounds of professional education should they possess?

> A precise description of the teachers needed to implement this program would be hazardous. However, certain common characteristics would greatly assist persons working in a program considerate of differences among the various children. A first understanding, and a most vital one for a teacher to possess, is a thorough committment to the dignity of individuals. Teachers must realize not only that children have varying interests and perceptions of the world in which they perform, but that each of these varied perceptions needs to be respected. If the child is allowed sufficient freedom of expression to illustrate clearly how he perceives his environment, the teacher will be better able to identify the distortions which the child may have and, in this manner, establish highly personal learning objectives designed to assist the child in his adjustments to the learning setting and the social world in which he lives.

Such indications of needs for children will not be made available to the teacher unless she demonstrates sincere respect for children's separate views. Secondly, each teacher or para-professional needs to be thoroughly aware of non-directive techniques of instruction. Although detailed discussions will be presented relative to this methodology in a later chapter, it would be well to understand at this point that such techniques would include all of the devices of instruction that will free the child to express himself in all possible media. These techniques will include skills in nondirective questioning, methods of demonstrating receptive listening, and skills of rapport building with individual children. Thirdly, teachers possessing a deep interest in all of the elements of their environment and the activities which take place in their social world, will convey this enthusiasm for life to the children. Such attitudes toward life will encourage the children to explore and freely direct their interests in equally broad fields.

5. *In the structure of this form of learning, are there no common beginning points for all children in the class?*

The reader might follow this question with another which asks, "Should there be common starting points in the processes of learning?" In truth there is a critical need for educators to understand that learning to read and communicate in the language of the school does not begin when the child enters the classroom. The skills of learning and the varying degrees of participation in these processes have been acquired long before the child enrolls in the "beginning readiness" program. There is an equal need for teachers to understand that the processes of communication have been highly developed for the majority of children before they have reached school age.[3] In a program that assumes the importance

---

[3] Walter D. Loban, *The Language of Elementary School Children*, Research Report No. 1, (Champaign, Illinois, National Council of Teachers of English, 1963).

of taking children through the prescribed steps in the "learning to read" program, definite beginnings are established for all children, at least in theory. In fact, however, children begin this study either much before the school introduces it or somewhat later than teachers would like them to. The major differences in a formalized, total class program of instruction in reading and language development and the individualized approach presented in this text have to do with recognition of the varied levels which children have achieved by the time they enter school. The formal approach assumes that this is the beginning point for all. The language experience methods assume that much has taken place prior to entry into school and capitalizes upon these prior learnings.

6. *In this program, will each child follow a course of learning which will be unique when compared with courses other students are following?*

This is possible, although unlikely. Peer guidance and social position have much to do with learning for children at any age. What Bill does may be highly attractive to many other students in the class, as much because they can see that Bill enjoys his experiences as because they are interested in the same field of study. Therefore, through natural leadership and a freedom of choice, each child may frequently follow the courses established by others. The choice of this course of action must be the child's, however. As will be discussed later, there will be frequent illustration of common needs among children. These may relate to word attack skills, writing skills, or other important tools to be implemented in a process of developing more sophisticated communication techniques. It is important, though, to note that each of the several children with common weaknesses in his "tool box" may be performing at a more advanced or slower pace than others with whom he is grouped for the study of specific skills. The fact that each has a need in common with other students in the class is too often the only consideration in the grouping process. It may be that once this particular need is corrected, there will be no further occasion for a similar grouping of these particular children.

7. *Inasmuch as boys and girls have unique patterns for learning coupled with unique areas of interest, would it be better to group boys separately from girls as has been characteristic in some European school systems?*

Although it is possible to note specific advantages in program separation for boys and girls, such action would also have an even greater number of disadvantages. Perhaps the most noteworthy of the disadvantages would have to do with the limitations placed upon each sex when they are forced to function in an all-male or all-female environment. It will be remembered that boys have large numbers of unique interests, but, also, that boys share with girls many other interests. Moreover, girls are somewhat more versatile and quite able to function well in a male environment. To restrict the child to an environment which is singularly male or female would have the same detrimental effects found in a sex-dominant setting. Educators would do well to consider the dangers of searching for "mechanical" solutions to instructional problems. Simply grouping children in new patterns, scheduling instruction for boys in different modes from girls, and making other similar arrangements will have little if any real effect upon learning patterns. The really necessary changes must take place in the manner in which children are directed through programs. In a stimulating setting, children with the freedom to make choices in courses of action can make substantially better progress than would be expected in classrooms where expectations of conformity for all children exist. The damage is done when boys are expected to conform to the patterns established in a feminine classroom.

8. *Is it to be assumed that inter-personal relationships between the child and*

the teacher are more important to learning than the mastery of skills in language or reading programs?

> This assumption is absolutely valid. Without the foundation of a good working relationship, a relationship based upon strong mutual respect, the teacher cannot expect the child to progress properly. If such a close relationship does not exist, it can be said that "learning is in spite of the teacher" rather than because of her. Also, a close relationship with others in his environment will assist in making the child feel good about his position, consequently helping him in the learning processes.

A study of learning processes and perceptual differences is sufficiently complex that the reader must accept the remarks in this chapter as introductory only. Further study can be done through the use of the references provided below.

REFERENCES

Association for Supervision and Curriculum Development. *Individualizing Instruction*, Ronald C. Doll, editor. 1964 Yearbook Committee, Washington, D.C.: A.S.C.D. 1964.

Perceiving Behaving Becoming, Arthur W. Comb, Chairman, 1962 Yearbook Committee, Washington, D.C.: A.S.C.D. 1964.

Grambs, Jean D. and Walter B. Waetjen. "Being Equally Different", *The National Elementary Principal*, 46: 59–67 November, 1966.

Loban, Walter D., *The Language of Elementary School Children*, Research Report No. 1. Champaign, Illinois: National Council of Teachers of English, 1965.

Wyatt, Nita M., "The Reading Achievement of First Grade Boys versus First Grade Girls," *The Reading Teacher*, 19: 661–665, May 1966.

chapter three

Specific differences in language development between boys and girls

That language growth should be viewed as one of the several extensions of personality was treated briefly in Chapter 2.[1] Encouraging individuality in the development of one's personality is not a foreign concept to educators in the public school system. Seeing language development as an expression of personality may well be new to many teachers, however.

It would be redundant to make further remarks about the growth of personality and the wholesome environments necessary to bring about the healthy characters desired. Inasmuch as this work treats language and reading development, further attention will not be given to the strengthening of personalities, per se. However, as language is an expression of personality, the reader may wish to examine further some of the writings in this field. It is sufficient to note that language is just one of the many personality expressions and, although it is discussed independently in this chapter, it is fundamental to the precepts presented to recognize that language is not a foundation quality in itself, but rather an outward manifestation of the person.

[1] California State Department of Education, *English Language Framework for California Public Schools*, (Sacramento, California, 1968) p. 9.

Language and the person

Moreover, it is essential to recognize that man's greatest accomplishment—that which sets him apart from lower forms of animals—is his facility with language. The abilities to express one's inner self through a commonly understood media which possesses the flexibility necessary for inclusion of the complete spectrum of individuality in man makes this accomplishment magnificent. Having achieved such a lofty goal, it would be nothing short of criminal to standardize and restrict language expression to reflect only the personalities of language "experts."

Language must also be viewed as a growing form of expression. Like building blocks, language is "reborn" and enlarged upon with each succeeding generation. The world in which each child must live and interact is recognized as constantly changing and the processes of interaction, including language expression, must change in like manner. Vygotsky makes two profound statements appropriate to this discussion.[2] He states that, "The relation of thought to word is not a thing, but a process, a continual movement back and forth from thought to word and from word to thought." Also, "Thought is not merely expressed in words; it comes into existence through them."

Assuming the correctness of Vygotsky's statements, then, it must be accepted that for a child to think about his environment, he must formulate his thoughts through the use of language. To restrict or formalize his freedom in the use of language is to restrict his ability to think and interact in his environment.

During the earliest years of a child's development, the progress which he makes in language expression is recognized by others, particularly the child's parents and siblings, as worthy of respect and rewarding encouragement. As the child continues his progress, he also begins to take delight in his accomplishments. Although it is accepted that much of this development is through the processes of imitation, the child does not view his achievement in language as being other than personal in nature. His experimentations and acceptance of patterns of expression are closely allied with his adventures in his environment.

[2] Lev Semenovich Vygotsky, *Thought and Language*, (Cambridge, Massachusetts, M.I.T. Press, 1962) p. 195.

Only two prominent restrictions are placed upon the child as he ventures into language. The first is the almost always constant restriction to the use of socially acceptable forms of language. "Almost always" because sometime desired reactions are gained through the use of "naughty" language. The second restriction is generally related to the sex of the child. Boys are encouraged to express themselves in forms which are masculine in character. Girls are less restricted in this matter. Therefore, boys learn to understand the language of both sexes, but most frequently distinguish between their manner of speech and the speech form used by their female counterparts. Girls use both the boys' and the girls' language forms. A third, although relatively less permanent restriction, is the limitation in many homes in the use of language for expression. Although this latter restriction handicaps the child temporarily, once the child enters the active language world, with adequate help he soon develops equal facility in this form of expression with his associates. The two major restrictions upon language development must, however, be viewed as permanent influences upon the functional scope of a child's facility in this media.

Factors influencing language development

Certain other factors influence the early development of language abilities in individual children. Although generally none of these factors provide permanent restrictions upon the child, each has a part to play in a study of language growth.

Perhaps most prominent among the several other influencing factors is the degree to which the home environment is accepting, affectionate and nonpunitive of the explorations of the child. As mentioned in preceding chapters, recognition of the dignity of the individual and his rights of expression is essential. When such recognition is made in the very earliest years of the child's life, language growth is substantially unimpeded.

The mother's role in language development must be considered as another factor either limiting or expanding language growth. The closeness of the relationships between the child and his mother—not necessarily the amount of love which each possesses for the other, but the amount of "expressed love"—has much to do with the progress which the child makes in language facility. A tense, anxious mother may, through her actions, actually impede the development of language in her child. The ability of the child and his mother to hold unrestricted conversations on common levels provides much of the initial stimulus for language growth. Unfortunately, such communication opportunities are more frequent for girls than they are for boys. Active, robust, perhaps even rowdy outdoor activities, preclude the normal full participation of mother and child in the instances of boys. Girls more often than not are guided into the types of activities in which the mother may participate fully. This rejection on the part of mothers of the activities and opportunities for communication with their sons, although not intended, affects the early stimulus of language. For this reason, it may appear that girls have more native ability than do boys. Acceptance of this *appearance of superiority* on the part of girls can be more dangerous to educators than the actual variations which exist in language growth between the sexes.

As mentioned earlier, societal expectations for boys and girls differ. These expectations must be viewed as restrictive to boys' growth in language. Expressions in the form of physical action are much more to be condoned, even encouraged, in boys than they are in girls. "*Sitting*" *conversations* are not considered to be masculine, but feminine in character.

Life patterns for boys, then, differ from those of girls during the years prior to school. Because of these differences, it is assumed that boys enter school in a somewhat retarded state of language development. However, numerous studies in the field of language indicate that this is not the case. In fact, these studies substantiate the fact that boys and girls are equally able in language performance. Assumptions that boys are retarded in their language growth patterns leads educators to expect girls to outperform boys. Boys are expected to be slow in language achievement. These expectations, based upon false assumptions, do serious harm to boys.

Assumptions made with regard to the performance abilities in language of boys when compared to girls tend to be reinforced during the early months of school life for children. Girls do, in fact, achieve at a more rapid rate than do boys in the field of reading and language development. This is not because girls have greater verbal abilities than their male counterparts. Rather, this seeming superiority appears through a combination of circumstances, each serving to further handicap boys.

First, the assumptions made that boys are slower than girls in language growth in itself serves to restrict the boys. Teachers "knowing" that it is proper to expect girls to perform better than boys will find their expectations fulfilled. In making such determinations, teachers frequently delay the beginning reading program for boys accordingly. The retardation, then, is imposed by the teacher and not by the boys.[3] Further, it has been determined that children tend to perform much in accord with what is expected of them by the teacher in the classroom.

An interesting anecdote illustrates just how well children follow what is expected of them.

The setting was a first grade class in which a boy named Tom was performing in accord with the teacher's expectations for a "normal" child of his age.

At the close of each day, another boy of fifth grade placement came by to pick up Tom before going home. This disturbed Tom's teacher after some time because it just did not seem proper for the older boy to be so attached to a younger child.

At the close of one day and upon the arrival of the fifth grade child, the teacher asked the older boy several questions.

"Why do you wait for Tom each day? Does he live by you? Does he play ball with you after school?"

Tom's older friend said, "No, Tom does not live near me. He's my friend and he reads to me."

The somewhat startled teacher thought that this was most unlikely inasmuch as Tom was struggling to some extent in the first reader in her classroom.

Further pursuit of the issue, however, turned up the information that Tom was presently reading "Robinson Crusoe" to the older boy and could do so with ease. In the classroom, though, he thought that this was not what the teacher expected of him.

Secondly, existing school programs are structured in such a manner as to be more readily adapted to the feminine background of students. The vocabulary and habits of boys developed through their environment is just not "school-like," and therefore the boys have an additional handicap.

Moreover, instruments used to measure the progress made by

[3] Robert Rosenthal and Lenore F. Jacobson, "Teacher Expectations for the Disadvantaged," *Scientific American*, Vol. 218, Number 4, (April, 1968) pp. 19–23.

children are standardized upon the past experiences of children in school. Because of the feminine character of the school program, such instruments tend to perpetuate the superior position of girls in the scores made.

The combination of lower expectations, assumed needs for delay in starting a reading development program, the feminine character of the school, and standardized instruments for measurement based upon all of the previous determinations, tend to severely handicap the male student in language growth. The school system seems neither to be anticipating the needs nor the true potentials of children, especially boys, when they enter school. Rather, improper determinations are made with regard to the character of incoming students and a program constructed upon these shaky premises. Relationships between the school program and children are formed on a group basis, with little regard for individual variations in abilities and potentials. Interests of the individual child are subordinated to those of the group, and it is in this approach that much of the serious harm is done.

Interests and vocabulary development

By ignoring the particular interests of each child, especially the interests of boys, the school fails to capitalize upon built-in readiness for the communication skills. (By ignoring these interests, many boys are lost in the early stages of formal schooling.) Some are lost forever. Many fill the remedial classes and suffer the stigma of a language handicap throughout their years in the educational system.

Interests of children can be illustrated by a simple sampling technique. Collecting the stories of first grade children—or children at any level, for that matter—will provide samplings of the topical variations in children's interests. Further examination of these stories will clearly illustrate differences even in vocabulary used. These stories may be written by the children or told to a teacher and recorded for the child. In the following brief sampling, such variations and commonly used nouns demonstrate the case in point.

Common terms: (Nouns used by both girls and boys.)

house   goose

milkman	bugs
airplane	honey
witch	badger
skunk	squirrel

Terms used mainly by girls:

movies	garden
candy cane	sky
rabbit	apple
dolly	pumpkin
chalkboard	

Terms used mainly by boys:

robot	wagon
monster	treasures
racing track	monkey
groundhog	truck
fist	gun
machine	factory

Although this informal sampling is brief and is only the product of one such examination of first grade children and the language they use, it does indicate sharp differences between boys and girls.

The reader may, also, from the listing given, note which words would more likely be found in the approved school program. Whereas few, if any, of the girls' terms would be considered inappropriate to stories written in school, several of the terms selected for use by boys would meet with disapproval from many teachers.

An interesting study was made by Preston relative to reading achievement in German and American schools.[4] Preston found that, "While the (test) means of American girls exceeded those of American boys at both grade level studies (Grades 4 and 6), the reverse was true

[4] Ralph C. Preston, "Reading Achievement of German and American Children," *School and Society*, Vol. 90.

in the German sample." Preston accounts for this difference by the fact that in German schools more male teachers are employed and masculine activities and interests gain greater acceptance. This study seems to further strengthen the premise presented in this chapter that the school places the restrictions upon boys in the American system; the handicaps are not necessarily inherent among male students.

Aside from teacher or educational system impositions made upon the boys with regard to printed language, studies show that actual syntactical differences do occur between the sexes. O'Donnel, Griffin, and Norris substantiate this in the following statement.[5]

Numerous differences were observed in structures and functions in the language of boys and girls at the sixth grade levels studies, and a good many of them were large enough to be statistically significant. In speech, however, the differences so fluctuated that no distinct, consistent pattern was indicated.

Disregarding the restrictions of the printed forms of language, then, and considering only the speech structures of boys and girls, it would seem that sex is not a factor. However, when written language is examined, girls appear to be clearly superior to boys. That each sex is equal to the other in oral language, but that differences occur in the written form, would indicate strongly that the inferior position of boys is the fault of the instructional program.

Sex role identification in language development

The abilities of girls which allow them to adapt more easily to structured environments, prescribed programs, and the other features of the formal school setting should also be considered. The adjustments required of the child entering school are largely related to the qualities of adaptiveness. Perhaps it is because girls have been given substantially more training in "proper conduct" by parents. It may be because of other environmental pressures in the years prior to entering the school system. The fact is, though, that girls are able to make rapid adjustments to the instructional setting. Boys, in general,

[5] Roy C. O'Donnel, William J. Griffin and Raymond C. Norris, *Syntax of Kindergarten and Elementary Children: A Transformational Analysis*, National Council of Teachers of English, NCTE Committee on Research, Bulletin No. 8, p. 96.

do not do so well when these rapid adjustments are expected in structured environments.

Rapid adjustments to the school setting may be a matter of *desire*. Whereas girls may find it easy to shift from the *mother model* to the *female teacher model*, boys may find it substantially more difficult to shift from the *father model* to the *female teacher model*. The period just prior to the initial entry into school at ages four or five provides a time when the ties between father and son are usually the strongest. An abrupt separation or shifting of models at this stage in life cannot help but be difficult.

The teacher must not only be aware of the differences which frequently exist in the sex models for boys, but also must examine the functional restrictions or stimulus of the different models. Girls receive careful "coaching" from their parents, particularly the mother, in language habits. Because of this formal styling of language in the period before school, adjustments are facilitated to the language of the school.

Fathers, serving as male models for their sons, are far less interested in formal expression. In fact, it is not uncommon for fathers and sons to communicate in nonverbal forms. When language is used, however, abbreviated sentences, creative word forms, and single words frequently serve all of the communication requirements between fathers and their sons. The speech patterns of men are generally less structured, even when they are talking to others of adult age. Therefore, boys imitating the communication patterns of male adults, will find that their models do not speak the school language. Adjustments to the instructional program are further handicapped as a result.

Although there is a lack of sufficient research to support the following phenomenon, it would seem to be true. Associations among the female members of society, or in mixed sex groups, appear to be largely upon a verbal basis. Active oral communication is frequently the foundation of such associations. In a male society, communication is as frequently nonverbal in form as verbal. Mothers and daughters or mothers and sons establish close association through oral communication. In the male society, oral communication is not required. Strangely, the more closely allied the members of a male community are, the less oral communication appears necessary. This occurs between father and son in relationships which are very close. It is not so unusual, then, that adjustments to feminine school settings are difficult.

Vygotsky discusses a form of communication which is closely allied to the non-oral communication of a male society.[6] This form of speech Vygotsky refers to as *inner* or *predictive speech*. In his discussions of this form of communication, Vygotsky compares such a process to the processes of writing draft papers and the stages of refinement to a final draft form. Inner speech is comparable to the idea communication found in the first draft of a writing. Sentence structures are disconnected and incomplete. Ideas are paramount and the formulation of these ideas in the mental processes is refined only enough to permit the subject to communicate with himself. The formalized, final draft of oral communication used with others is not necessary when communication is only with one's self. How does this relate to the male nonlanguage communication? It would appear that the more non-oral forms of communication are used, as in the case in a father and son association, the more likely *predictive forms of communication* will become conditions of language development. Such predictive forms of language will become used, even in vocalized or written expressions. The degree to which such egocentric communication is conditioned in the oral or written responses of male students will be the degree to which these students will have difficulty with the language of the classroom.

Such *inner speech* forms of communication as presented by Vygotsky are not restrictive of "idea" communications, however. The difficulty arises in communicating these thoughts into acceptable, school language. There is a real possibility for students using predictive language to communicate far more ideas through the use of such communication forms, but placing these ideas into acceptable classroom language restricts, and perhaps offends, the user of this communication style. Male students, conditioned to non-oral media, tend to disregard precision in meaning and reject the formal structures of language taught in the classroom.

Implications for the instructional program

1. *If we accept the fact that boys are often somewhat restricted in language development and appear to be less verbal than girls, how can we help boys to develop greater facility in the use of language?*

[6]Lev Semenovich Vygotsky, *Thought and Language*, Cambridge, Mass.: The M.I.T. Press, 1962.

First, it is important that teachers realize that sometimes assumptions are made about the verbal capabilities of boys when, in fact, they are equally capable in verbal skills, but simply do not wish to function orally in a feminine atmosphere. This may be a matter of boys' perceptions of the expected form or standard for verbalization in school. Or it may be that boys find little to discuss in the environment of the school. To reduce or eliminate the handicaps for verbal expression in the classroom, teachers must make adequate provisions for boys to utilize their own forms of expression without unnecessary restriction. Accepting the form of language used by each child is of fundamental importance to developing programs of language instruction. Moreover, it is vital that boys understand that what they wish to talk about is important. A sincere interest on the part of the teacher in topics of interest to boys will do much to stimulate this free expression. Further, it is helpful if the teacher makes provisions for engaging in individual conversations with boys. Boys, more often than girls, prefer private discussions on topics related to their special interests. Verbalization begun on an individualized basis will soon permit expansion to group or class presentations by the boys. Finally, it is vitally important that opportunities to talk about something be provided. This may be a matter of the teacher listening in on conversations between boys and selecting topics worthy of presentation or further discussion, either in an individual meeting with the teacher or in presentation to the class. Frequently these discussion topics will be related to firsthand experiences. Another approach is to include items of particular interest to boys in classroom displays or collections. These items can readily serve as discussion centers for initiating the verbal growth desired.

2. *A tense, anxious mother may impede the language development of a boy and a tense, anxious teacher may further this handicap to language development.*

What can the teacher do to relieve tensions that arise in relation to reading and language development?

Forcing a child to perform in any predetermined manner, whether in relation to language or any other learning function, can have damaging effects. Expecting a boy to function in accord with some reading or language standard or form will prevent growth in communication skills. This may be avoided through the use of a variety of techniques. First, make it possible for the boy to have choices in the manner and times for verbalizing. If the student knows that he can participate when he wants to and does not have to perform in accord with the dictates of the teacher, much will be done to reduce these tensions. Allowing a number of alternate forms of expression will also assist in the solution of this problem. For example, boys may prefer to express themselves through construction of demonstration models or exhibits rather than in written form. Also, some will prefer expressions of ideas through the use of music, art materials or rhythmic activities. In this regard it should be remembered that boys are more active and energetic than girls and may wish to express themselves through games and outdoor activity. Each of these factors, or combinations of them, may be used in the reduction of tensions and the development of natural expression among boys.

3. *When teachers expect boys to be retarded in language development, such expectations may influence performance. How can teachers avoid this eventuality?*

It is best to begin by knowing as much about each boy's particular interests and capabilities as is possible. Upon the abilities of each boy can be built programs of instruction designed to capitalize upon positive qualities rather than correct expected weaknesses. In this light, it will help greatly to work with each child individually as much as is possible. Further, it is important to avoid the pitfalls of ability grouping in teaching reading and language skills. This form of patterned instruction tends to formalize negative assumptions about the abilities of boys. Designing programs around the intense interests of boys will further help to reduce predetermined expectations for performance. Moreover, it is helpful if the elements of competition can be removed from the classroom environment. Such factors, including the use of extrinsic rewards, tend to restrict further the performance levels for all children, but particularly for boys. The important concept to be accepted by teachers and conveyed to boys is that they are important and are welcome members of the class because of what they can contribute, not that they are in the class because of all the things which they cannot do in accord with some standard.

4. *How can teachers help boys make a smooth transition from the home environment to the school situation?*

This is, of course, a broad question and an adequate answer would require a great deal of space. In brief, however, there are techniques which will provide a partial response to the question. It is important, first, for the teacher to understand and accept the very real differences between boys and girls in relation to the individual self-perception of each child. Going beyond this, though, provisions can be made to include books and reading materials that depict characters with whom the boy can readily identify and characters with a male image consistent with his self-concept. This will require knowing something about each boy entering the classroom. Also, the teacher may find it helpful to encourage fathers and older brothers to visit in the classroom. Their interest in the activities of the classroom may make the functions of the classroom take on new meaning for the boy in a manner consistent with his male image. Capitalizing upon male members of the teaching staff or administrators as friends of the boys will also further the cause of providing solutions to the problem of transition from home to school.

REFERENCES

California State Department of Education, *English Language Framework for California Public Schools*. Sacramento: 1968.

Committee of the National Conference on Research in English, *Factors That Influence Language Growth*, Dorothy McCarthy, Chairman. Champaign, Illinois: National Council of Teachers of English, 1952.

Holt, John, *How Children Fail*. New York: Dell Publishing Co., 1964.

Irwin, Theodore, "Boy–Girl Differences—Inborn or Acquired?" *Parents' Magazine*, 43: 40–41, 64–65, July 1968.

Waetjen, Walter B., and Grambs, Jean D., "Sex Differences: A Case of Educational Evasion?" *Teachers College Record*, 65: 261–71, December 1963.

Vygotsky, Lev Semenovich, *Thought and Language*. Cambridge, Mass.: The M.I.T. Press, 1962.

chapter four

Imposed language standards and the male image

The enormous forces pressing upon the personality of each individual throughout his life serve to shape, redirect, or restrict the expressions of personal uniqueness. A number of these forces—home, neighborhood, friends, and counselors, including the minister and the family doctor—have been recognized by educators for many years. Others have only recently been regarded as influences of deciding quality. Some, in particular, have much to do with the communicative abilities of children.

As noted earlier in this work, the influences of the home, particularly of the parents, have been presented. The verbal qualities of each child's earliest environment are still recognized as highly significant to progress in language for the individual. However, inasmuch as the language influences of the home have been long recognized by educators as having a large part in the course of language development, further discussion will not be given to this factor in this chapter, except as it is related to other factors discussed.

Socio-economic environment and language development

Recently, recognition has been given to the fundamental influences of the socio-economic environment of the child. Characteristically, the schools and instructional materials have been structured around the concepts of the middle class, suburban, or small-town America. Upon this foundation, assumptions of "proper" language patterns have been utilized in structuring the format of reading and language textbooks. That such a structure is common to the experiential backgrounds of large numbers of students, cannot be debated. Universal acceptance of these assumptions is not, however, educationally wise for all children. With the increasing urbanization of the population, corresponding allowances for variations in backgrounds must be made.

Accepting Bloom's research, which substantiates that children acquire more than half of their intelligence by the age of four, and assuming that for many children this growth takes place in an environment of the impoverished core city, it is not difficult to understand the inappropriateness of "small-town" textbooks. The language of these books is not related to even the polite language of the ghetto. Neither are the settings for the stories, the tree-lined streets of the pictures, or the middle-class characters of the books related to the real-life climate in which many children live. In fact, in many instances, even the clean, bound book is strange. The imposition of this totally unrelated textual environment is not considerate of the prior experiences of the children.

The ghetto is largely male oriented. Physical strength and manly language dominate this setting. Consequently, an adjustment to the fundamentally "clean" setting of the classroom, with a feminine dominance, is simply not possible or consistent with existing male images. Girls, too, adopt the maleness of the central city environment and they, too, have more difficult adjustments to make than do their suburban counterparts.

Although not necessarily sex linked, another factor is of critical importance to the adaptations required of ghetto children when they enter school. This element has to do with the essentially aggressive quality of life in the core city. To survive and grow as an individual in this climate requires the child to be action oriented, to be aggressive. Schools are passive in climate and impose a conforming pattern upon students, if they are to be successful. The conflicting roles which pupils must play during their school years is most damaging to children, especially to boys. While in school during the day, they must be passive to succeed: with the close of the school day, aggressiveness is demanded if personal status is to be achieved.

The gross culture of the core city influences the lives of all children living in this environment. However, within the larger culture of the city are numerous smaller cultural segments, each providing the child with various assets and handicaps with respect to growth in the school program.

The pervading impression of poverty upon the lives of large numbers of children restricts severely their language growth. In this atmosphere of limited verbalization, either in printed or spoken form, the vocabulary and speech patterns of children fail to mature. Much of the language development is along lines of life in the ghetto and, thus, is totally unacceptable in the school. The male student is more likely to reflect such a pattern. In other respects, the language of the core city is unique to the setting and has no relevance to the "proper" language of the textbooks. The development of language patterns along these lines does not assist the child to prepare for learning in the classroom. It can be said that the years before school are lost with respect to language readiness for education in the school. Poverty handicaps language development.

The educational system and language

As mentioned, the language of the school is suburban or small-town in character. Moreover, the language of the educational system is consistent with the dominant ethnic culture of the nation. Minority ethnic cultures, with their corresponding language differences, are not considered in the classroom. To the extent that a child is an active representative of his minority culture, the language patterns he uses handicap his educational growth. Students from homes which commonly use patterns of mixed English and non-English systems of communication or, more particularly, children from non-English-speaking homes, are especially handicapped. Only recently have a few states legalized instruction in other than the English language in order to develop programs considerate of large numbers of non-English-speaking students. Many children, growing up in the confines of a predominantly minority ethnic culture, have not even heard standard school language prior to entry into school.

It is necessary that educators understand, also, that the handicaps to language growth are not all related to the limitations of prior language. Many of the restrictions are fundamentally related to the value systems commonly accepted in the environment in which the child lives, particularly his home.

Because of the unrelatedness of the school setting, the learnings of the system, and the unrealistic goals of the educational structure, many minority groups simply say, "It's not for us." By this they mean that schools are for the middle-class, white student. In this process of rejecting the programs of the school, little is done to develop the attitudinal qualities which suburban children acquire to assist them in the adjustments which they must make upon entry into the school system. If these qualities of indifference are not fully realized before the minority, ghetto child reaches school age, they are soon brought home to him when he discovers that he cannot perform successfully in the existing structure. Understanding of this quality is frequently lacking in the present school system.

Van Atta, in her discussion of the ghetto school, quotes from taped interviews of core-city citizens.[1]

Our kids have never had a chance to develop their own potential. There have been too many persons with missionary zeal, who say, 'Poor little dears. They don't have what I have and let's help them get it and make it as comfortable and as nice for them as we can and keep them happy.'

This is like putting clothes on a native. Having sympathy for and empathy for are two different things and too many teachers have more sympathy than empathy. They don't have the understanding, but you can't hold this against them because no one's doing anything to tell them anything...

Many teachers have never experienced failure, so how will they know how to deal with kids that are failing all the time. We have teachers who have never had a problem that wasn't solved or didn't have the potential for being solved . . . how can they handle people that have problems that can't be solved?

You've got to know what these kids are up against.

[1] Grace Van Atta, "Like It Is—Pressures in a Ghetto School," *Theory Into Practice: Pressures on Children*, Vol. VII, Number 1, (February, 1968), (College of Education, The Ohio State University), pp. 17–22.

In this discussion it can be seen that many children have severe environmental and cultural handicaps and that they are frequently confronted with a system which fails to recognize that these handicaps do, in fact, exist.

The teacher and language development

The school demonstrates its irrelevance to the environments of children in a vast number of ways—many of these demonstrations having devastating effect upon the growth of the individual.

First, and most obvious, the limitations upon the form and style of language imposed by the teacher must be noted. Not only must the child develop the skills of understanding this frequently "foreign" speech pattern, but he must also adopt this pattern if he is to succeed.

This process of imposing a style of language upon the students of a classroom has the effect of closing the opportunities for communication. Success in the educational system will not come about unless the processes of communication between the child and the teacher are founded upon skills and understandings which each feels the other is capable of accepting. If the language expected in the classroom is not the language which the child understands, or is capable of using, then there will be no effective communication.

Secondly, the imposition of a school language upon students not normally comfortable with this form of communication sharply attacks the child's concept of self. He must reject his own speech pattern for that used in the school. In doing so, he rejects the language patterns of his parents and associates outside of the school. Frequently the boy would prefer to maintain his out-of-school language, even though this may mean failure in the classroom. If the child is to feel good about himself, and he must if he is to succeed in any endeavor, it is important that he be accepted in his entirety. This includes his language habits.

Alert teachers, using all of their perceptive skills, will recognize the fundamental importance of accepting children as they are, not because they are adequate as they are, but because they must feel that they are adequate for acceptance by others. This may actually be painful to the well-trained teacher, but she knows the importance of such acceptance to the learning processes.

Educators use a variety of techniques, some of them most indirect, to demonstrate acceptance or rejection of children's language patterns. Some, also, are not intentional. Of course, the most direct of these is to simply tell the boy that his speech is not acceptable or wrong in the school. This can be terribly damaging.

Overcorrecting the speech habits of children can have the same effect. This is not as direct as telling him bluntly that his language is not good, but soon he gets this message. The overcorrection of either written work or oral reading will also transmit this message. It might be said, incidentally, that in an "around the circle" reading group, other children may be correcting a student in the same manner with the same negative results. The child soon learns to communicate as little as possible to avoid exposing himself to such treatment.

Many other habits or techniques used by the teacher will restrict a child's language. A simple, derisive smile, or a raised eyebrow when the pupil expresses himself in other than "proper English" will quickly convey to the students his mistake. Oral correction is not needed to gain the negative effect.

Not engaging children in mutually accepting conversation also transmits the feelings of rejection to children. Unfortunately, this is easy for the teacher to do with large numbers of students in the class-room. The quiet, rejected child is simply overlooked. Even performing at his very best, the teacher can temporarily damage the ego of a child. It is important, then, to be continuously aware of the many ways in which the damage may be done.

Educators have, for years, had philosophical fun with their debate on what is "proper" or "standard" English. Implied in this debate is the question of "acceptable" English. Entering into this philosophical exercise in relation to "acceptable" English would not be appropriate here. However, the seemingly harmless or well-intentioned accept-ance of a so-called standard English will provide the foundation for much serious damage to the ego of verbally handicapped children, especially boys who would much prefer to communicate meanings rather than speak in grammar school terms.

In the search for norms which would simplify the functions which the teacher must perform, artificial standards are used. The norm for English usage, norms for minimum grade-level performance, norms for measurement, norms for acceptable conduct, and a multitude of other artificial measurements all interfere substantially with the full acceptance of children, especially those children deviating markedly from the so-called norm. Because of the fundamentally feminine character of the language of the school, the median measure forces boys into a much more unfavorable position. Moreover, the search for standard measures leads the teacher further and further from her basic guideline: that of accepting fully all children with whom she works. Love and affection for children, empathy with students, and a genuine desire to be associated with each pupil cannot be prestructured in accord with norms.

If teachers will utilize the full intent of the professional cliché which says, "accept children where they are when they arrive, and go from there," a remarkable revolution will take place in the classroom. Previously established standards for language, conduct, performance, and the other handicapping features of structured education would quickly disappear. Stress should be upon the word "accept," not upon the identification of the level which the child has reached in his educational ladder. Language is an expression of personality, and acceptance of this form of expression will greatly assist in paving the way to understanding between teacher and child. Upon this understanding can be built the structure of learning.

Implications for the instructional program

1. *Is it necessary for teachers to assume the language patterns used by children when communicating with them?*

> The response to this question is generally no. Teachers gain very little and may actually offend the pupils by "talking down" to them. Moreover, it will not be possible for the teacher to function correctly in the varying dialects of all of the children in her class. Teachers may, however, adopt patterns of speech which use brief sentence structures when conversing with children. Short oral sentences are much more easily understood by children just as abbreviated printed sentences quicken understanding in a well-written novel. This device will permit the teacher to use appropriate adult vocabulary

without losing the verbal contact with individual students.

Alert teachers also use a system of "dual" language when conversing with groups of children. That is, they present a statement in one form and then inoffensively restate the same concept in another manner. This requires great skill and perception upon the part of the teacher. Improperly applied, this device can become offensive to the children in the classroom.

As has been said often and as will be repeated, if a fundamentally sound rapport is established between the teacher and each of her children, the students will feel free to inform the teacher when they are not understanding the language which she is using.

2. *Although it may be possible for the teacher to avoid imposing language patterns and standards upon individual students in the classroom, how is it possible to avoid the impositions made by the textbooks which children must use?*

It is necessary first, to understand that there are a variety of ways to use the textual materials printed for use in the classroom. If it is assumed that sequentially developed textbooks must be used in the form and order in which they are presented, as in the case of basal readers, then impositions will be made regardless of the devices the teacher uses to adjust the language of the classroom to that which is meaningful to children. It is not necessary to utilize the format presented by authors of sequentially developed textbooks. Teachers may develop individualized programs of instruction centered upon the peculiar interests and capabilities of students and utilize the textbook—even the basal reader —as a reference or anthology. In this manner, the basic instruction is adjusted to the abilities and interests of children, yet there is appropriate use made of the books available in the classroom. In addition, teachers may allow the student to convert to his own form of language the meanings gained from reading in reference materials.

Acceptance of this translation will permit the students to express their understanding of the material read.

3. *How is it possible to teach children to read without using the formal structure of basal reading books, which would be imposing language patterns upon children?*

A number of individualized methods of beginning reading instruction have been developed that do not, in fact, use the basal reader system. The best known, and by far the most flexible and considerate of individual differences, is the use of a language experience approach. Extensive guideline materials are available to the teacher to assist her in developing and using this adjustable method in the classroom. Dr. R. Van Allen has published such materials and they are readily accessible to teachers interested in such materials.[2] Essentially, the use of a language experience method bases instruction upon the full utilization of speaking and listening skills. Each child brings such skills to school when he first enters, although some of the children are not so sophisticated as others. If the child is able to express orally, concepts and understandings which he has about his experiences, these expressions can be written on charts or upon paper for the child. His experiences can then be "read" back to the teacher or other students because these experiences are his. Upon this foundation, initial vocabulary is developed. Also, around these pupil-dictated teacher-written experiences, the child makes his first introductions to writing and reading activities. In a limited way and without full description of the methodology of this process, the reader can recognize that books are really nothing more than the printed expressions of the authors. Utilization of this flexible method simply allows the child to become his own author. Also, the use of this method permits the child to

[2] Roach Van Allen and Claryce Allen, *Language Experiences in Reading*, Levels I, II, III (Chicago, Encyclopedia Britannica Press, 1966).

choose the topics of his writing and not have these subjects imposed upon him by other authors, particularly
the adult authors of basal reading series.

4. *Should teachers accept any language used by children in school?*

If by this it is meant, does the teacher accept vulgar
street language in the classroom, consideration must be
given to the manner and levels in which such language is
used by the students. If the classroom is at a primary
level, then the answer is for the most part affirmative.
In many instances the language of the home or of the
neighborhood is rough and frequently shocking to the
middle-class teacher. It is, however, the common, out-
of-school language. Teachers will need to accept this
form of language until the child realizes that such
speech patterns and vocabulary are not the generally
used language of the school. For some children, especially boys, this may require a long time. Among older
children in the more advanced levels of the school, such
language need not be always accepted. Adequate
counseling and guidance by the teacher will direct the
child away from rough street language towards more
acceptable patterns and vocabularies. Teachers need to
use caution in the counseling and guidance techniques
used in redirecting vocabulary habits of students. If the
redirection undermines the rapport between the teacher
and the student, then such counseling will do more harm
than good. Such counseling should be individual and
not presented in such a manner as will be damaging
to the individual student's concept of self. It will be
remembered that real learning takes place in a nondirective atmosphere. Each pupil needs subtle guidance
to assist him in coming to the realization that the language patterns he is using are not the most effective.
Such individual realizations will bring about far more
lasting learnings and permanent changes in the speech
habits of the students.

5. *Is it wrong to provide a model in terms of language patterns and standards which will be based upon the American ideal of customary language found in the comfortable, middle-class communities of the nation?*

To provide a single model is essentially wrong, regardless of whether this model has to do with language or some other desired learning. To begin a learning in this frame prevents the child making a choice, and learning requires great freedom of choice. Several models in a presentation or learning environment may well assist the child, particularly if these models permit the child to see himself in a different light. All too often the models established for children are far beyond the functional level of the students.

It is, as has been mentioned, highly questionable whether education has, as yet, been able to determine the standard of excellence in language which might be selected for a model. A brief conversation with teen-agers will readily demonstrate the inadequacy which they feel is inherent in standard English. Perhaps it can be assumed that students are at variance with the standard English model which teacher's are most comfortable. This language may well not be the most appropriate for general usage. If the search for models is considered important to the language development of children, it would seem wise to establish highly dynamic language exhibits which will continually expand the child's functional language. Such ever enlarging models will permit the child to select freely terms which are most fitting to the pictures he wishes to express—perhaps, the models will encourage the children to freely invent words. In this way, the child can enjoy fully the adventure of language development without encountering prescriptions provided for him. Certainly, the variety of models should permit the children to explore the idiom of the core city, the venacular of the working world, and the unique languages of cultural subdivisions of our society. In much the same framework of freedoms as would be expected of an artist mixing the many variations of color to achieve his personal interpretations on canvas, so must the artist in language usage be free to select, blend, and create vocabularies appropriate for his use.

6. *Being cognizant of the inherent dangers of "over-correcting" children's language usage, what devices may be used to insure the students' progress in the development of language?*

It is important to recall that the use of language as a media of expression is essentially an oral function. Even in the writing process and, all too frequently, in the reading function, a kind of *subvocalizing* is used. Knowing this allows teachers to utilize the great resources of the oral form in learning environments. If children are permitted—in fact, encouraged—to test their thoughts in oral form with good listeners, the weaknesses in their expressions will generally become obvious to them. If the audience does not understand what is being expressed, especially when understanding is not at the level of "feeling" the mood of the speaker, then the forms of expression will not be satisfying to the child using them. Moreover, if a child cannot think of the words which will best express the experiences he wishes to relate, then he is the first to recognize his need for assistance. Upon this personal recognition can be based the language instruction which he needs. Boys, especially, will want to tell stories and talk about adventures without internally testing the language they wish to utilize. Remarks such as, "How do I say it?" and "You know what I mean," will be common expressions in the oral stories presented by boys. Patience in listening and stimulating questions will permit the teacher to develop the language skills of the boys while they are in the process of expressing their adventures to the class audience.[3]

[3] W. King, M. L. King, and C. S. Huck, "Teaching Critical Reading to Elementary School Children," *Reading Research Quarterly*, Vol. 3, Number 4, (Summer, 1968) pp. 435–98. (Newark, Delaware; International Reading Association).

The variety of devices, then, which permits children to test their language usage in oral discussion or presentation will present the teacher with the tools needed to insure language growth.

Stress should be placed upon stimulating environments in which the pupils may explore and utilize the many "languages" familiar to them. Further, the excitement of experiencing and learning should be such that children recognize their own needs for additional language. Moreover, provisions for children to test the effectiveness of their language should be always present in this environment. Language development is not directed by teachers, but rather is stimulated and helped to grow.

REFERENCES

Bloom, Benjamin S., "Learning for Mastery," *Evaluation Comment*, Los Angeles. U.C.L.A. Center for the Study of Evaluation of Instructional Programs, Vol, 1, No. 2, May 1968.

Broderick, Mary, "Creativity in Children," *The National Elementary Principal*, 46: 18–24, November 1966.

Hentoff, Nat, *Our Children Are Dying*, New York: The Viking Press Inc., 1966.

Moore, G. Alexander, Jr., *Realities of the Urban Classroom*, Garden City, New York: Doubleday and Company, 1967.

Pollack, Jack Harrison, "Are Teachers Fair to Boys?" *Today's Health*, 46: 21–25, April 1968.

Riessman, Frank, *The Culturally Deprived Child*, New York: Harper and Row, Publishers, 1962.

chapter five

A masculine curriculum and the place of the male model

To provide properly for sex differences in the classroom, serious consideration must be given to a reorientation of curriculum and instructional methodology. Broad suggestions for curriculum change and instructional methods and techniques considerate of sex differences will form the framework of Chapter 6. In the true sense, curriculum becomes instructional form. Instructional methodology becomes difficult to distinguish in curriculum structure. Understanding of the unity and yet separateness of each of these essentials is necessary to the success of the educational process.

Biological and perceptual basis for curriculum design

Devising a curriculum which possesses the necessary sex orientations in order to broaden the scope in a manner advantageous to both boys and girls is not a difficult task. Simple recognition of the differences in the needs of male and female students will, in itself, do much to initiate a curriculum with varied sex orientations. Such recognition, if fully accepted by teachers, will immediately vary the oneness of the instructional program and give movement in the direction of individualization of curriculum structures.

Knowing the biological differences which exist between boys and girls gives direction for some curriculum development. For example, knowing that boys have superior strength, respond in a stronger way to stimuli, produce more carbon dioxide, are more frequently left-handed, have a higher incidence of color blindness, and produce more energy, gives the educator guidance in curriculum preparation.[1]

Some of these elements and their pertinence to the development of curriculum can easily be recognized. For example, instruction relative to recognition of different colors in the early period in school obviously must be adjusted in accord with the incidence of color blindness among boys. Not making such provisions may place the teacher in a position of frustration and have a devastating effect upon boys. Adjusting of writing requirements to the left-handedness, which is much more common among boys than girls, is needed if the program is to be realistic. Some provisions in the curriculum for these factors of sex difference have been made in the present program of the schools.

Curriculum provisions appropriate to greater energy output, a higher metabolism rate, and greater response to stimuli are, however, rare. The consumption rate of topical and material allowances in the curriculum needs to provide for the substantially greater concentration of energy which boys apply to studies, particularly if such materials are relevant to their interests. Coupled with this, of course, is the higher metabolism rate of boys, producing study by "fits and spasms" results. A highly flexible curriculum, which allows for consuming interests of the male students, must be provided. This will include extensive, although not necessarily prolonged, studies in curriculum areas of high interest. Having one story or one book, or even just books, relative to a high-interest topic will not be sufficient. It is better to collect many books, a variety of relative items of realia, organize centers accepting of experimentation, and generally establish temporary laboratories for vicarious and real exploration. The application of instructional techniques cognizant of this biological variation will be treated in

[1] Walter B. Waetjen and Jean D. Grambs, "Sex Differences: A Case of Educational Evasion?", *Teachers College Record*, Vol. 65, (December 1963) University of Maryland, pp. 261–71.

Chapter 6. However, it might be said at this point that teachers will sometimes despair of formulating collections and building laboratories, only to have the boys jump from one consuming interest to another with great rapidity—sometimes returning to a prior interest soon after a laboratory has been dismantled. Couple this, too, with the longer-lasting interests of girls, which may be focused upon the same study as that of the boys. Just when it would be advisable to remove one environment in order to adjust to newly acquired interests and needs for boys, it will be discovered that some girls want the learning center continued for additional time. Teaching problems immediately become compounded.

Additionally, boys as a group have less endurance and therefore need more, and more frequent, rest intervals in the curriculum established. Predetermined lessons with increasingly complex sequences of study will produce a higher degree of unsuccessful completions among the boys. Intense studies of shorter intervals will produce better results. Particularly devastating are the semester or year-long sequences of single book programs.

Differences between the sexes are more than biological. Perceptual differences also occur.[2] It is known that girls more readily perceive the desires of the teacher than do boys and, consequently make adjustments to these perceptions. Also, girls tend to be more perceptive of group desires. Boys rely more heavily upon inner feelings for guidance. Because of these perceptual variations, group study of common topics is more appropriate and functional for girls. Boys need individualized programs more frequently. Although the goals of the group and individual studies may be similar, the curriculum leading to the accomplishment of these goals may be substantially varied. It should be remembered, however, that girls often function in the manner of boys, as was previously mentioned. The reverse is seldom true, but teachers may find it more advantageous to individualize instruction for all students in order to allow for the functionally male mode of perception common to both sexes which frequently occurs.

A coupling of the perceptual variations between the sexes and the biological endurance differences, will give further direction to educators in curriculum development. The "stop and start" characteristics of boys' studies prepare them for rapid adjustment to new and more

[2] Walter B. Waetjen and Jean D. Grambs, ibid.

novel situations. The curriculum can be devised to capitalize upon this factor. Girls, however, are far more comfortable with less noticeable change in the sequence of studies.

Recognition of this in a program of language studies will direct the educator to organize the curriculum in such a manner as to permit boys to learn to read or write about their particular interests of the moment. A language experience orientation in the curriculum allows for the stops and starts of the boys and yet provides opportunity for the girls to approach their language studies in a connected, sequential manner.

The ability of the boys as a group to make more rapid transfer in learnings, when compared to their feminine counterparts, permits the teacher to forego the connective instruction joining units of curriculum all too common in existing programs.[3] Male students are able to transfer writing skills to experimentation in science without teacher assistance. Such unions of studies are not necessary for the male students and, if included, may destroy interest in further learning at a time when the teacher feels most sure of her techniques.

A well-directed teacher may, in order to allow fully for the boys' interests in the novel and surprise elements of study, use care in her descriptions of course work. Although the teacher may carefully establish some of the behavioral goals with the students in the class, the units of study or the vast array of the steps used to attain these goals may be withheld to be discovered by the students. Keeping such a program in mind allows the educator immense freedom in curriculum organization.

Curriculum development considerate of individual differences among students will establish goals in terms of terminal behaviors desired. This, then, will be followed by the mustering of all possible resource materials and persons, upon which each student may draw for the support he needs to attain the goals. In the utilization of this laboratory approach to learning, it will be found that girls follow the more traditionally academic paths toward achieving the goals than do boys. Freedom of choice will be permitted for both sexes, however. Such a curriculum organization will permit the learning of the same content by a great variety of approaches, each with real consideration of sex differences among the students.

[3] M. M. Kostick, "A Study of Transfer: Sex Differences in the Reasoning Process," *Journal of Educational Psychology*, Vol. 45 (December, 1954) pp. 449–458.

The academic orientation commonly applied by female students helps in understanding the commonly accepted tenet that girls excel in reading when compared to boys. Only partially, though! Unfortunately, the approaches utilized in teaching reading appeal to girls more than they do to boys. Also, norms used in measuring this superior position among girls have a feminine orientation. Nevertheless, because of a desire to apply this tool more frequently, girls do maintain an advantage in reading skill.

Selection of curriculum content provides the educator with difficult tasks. In the past, attempts have been made to accomplish these tasks in a manner acceptable to both male and female interests. The result is the *unsexing* of the educational program! Although there is some unsupported evidence that girls can function in this neuter environment, vast amounts of carefully developed data demonstrate that boys want to function in a male setting. It will be recalled that Lecky's studies point out that "self-consistency" is very strong in the male of the species.[4] Boys want to be boys!

Sharply identified, male characteristics must be found in the broad curriculum developed. Such factors should be developed in recognition of the strong feelings for adventure, curiosity, and action which are common traits and interests for the boys. In the formation of these units of study, the boy can readily identify himself and, as a consequence, participate fully.

Stanchfield, in her California studies, clearly identifies areas of particular interest among boys.[5] In doing so, she also identifies areas in which the boys have little interest as a group. Specifically, male students have reading interests which include the following broad topics:

> outdoor life
> exploration and expeditions
> sports and games
> science fiction
> sea adventures

[4] Prescott Lecky, *Self-Consistency: A Theory of Personality*, (New York, The Shoe String Press, Inc., 1961) pp. 6–7.

[5] Jo. M. Stanchfield, "Differences in Learning Patterns of Boys and Girls," (Unpublished Lectures, Occidental College, undated). (Mimeographed).

Boys have the least interest in the following topical areas:

> music
> plays (even if related to an
>   interest area)
> art
> family and home life
> poetry

A customary approach to boys' interests has been to wrap these interests into traditional packages for presentation in the classroom. This will be treated further in the next chapter, but it should be noted at this point that boys may like adventure, but they may not want it presented in the form of poetry!

Stanchfield further found that the manner of presentation of topical interests had much to do with the acceptability of these topics among male students.[6] Characteristics of reading interests best liked by boys would include at least the following:

> unusual experiences
> excitement
> suspense
> liveliness and action
> surprise and unexpectedness
> fantastic, fanciful, or weird elements
> funny incidents

It can be said, then, that boys are interested in particular topics which are readily identified. Moreover, such topical interests must be presented in a manner which is consistent with the forms noted above. This formation is further refined when the educator recognizes the male orientation toward singular action and individual strength. Boys don't want the individual's place subordinated to that of the group. In sports, the role of one boy must stand out. In adventure, family groups are not satisfactory. Again the individual must be prominent.

Moreover, the male student characteristically has strong interest in the moral strength demonstrated by characters in his reading. Boys do not like to read about hatred, cruelty, fighting, brutality. Similarly, they do not want love, sadness, or related features to be overexpressed in the stories which they read. A seemingly contradictory quality is

[6] Jo. M. Stanchfield, ibid.

noted when it is recognized that boys feel emotions and personally want to express these feelings, perhaps more so than girls.

The clear identification of specific interests among boys gives the educator particular guidance in the formation of curriculum. It is most obvious that curriculum structures which omit these particular interests will not be considerate of the male student. Nor will such structures be functional in a learning environment in which boys are expected to progress in accord with their abilities.

The male model in the elementary school

Clearly identifying topical interests of boys with respect to the curriculum is of major importance to the overall progress which they will enjoy. It is further understood that such provisions will greatly strengthen the instructional program of the school. However, such variations in the curriculum structure are not sufficient recognition of the sex differences which exist. Provisions must be made for the further inclusion of male models to fully realize the potentials of the male students.

Traditionally, the curriculum has been viewed as that collection of printed materials, including instructional guides, courses of study, textbooks, and supportive materials, which collectively form the educational program. It has been assumed that these materials were, in fact, the essential resources necessary for an adequate learning environment. Evidence clearly demonstrates that other factors or elements have a place in the curriculum. Most relevant of these new elements is the male model.

In recent years, the need for male models has been seen in the programs of preschool education in impoverished communities. The inclusion of such models came as a result of a recognized void in the home situations of the students enrolled. Studies of the results of such male effectiveness upon the learning habits of the students, both for boys and for girls, indicates that a kind of magic takes place. Male teachers or their aides with a sincere commitment to the programs for helping young children are able to produce astonishing results. Boys respond far more effectively with such leadership than has been the case in similar classes with only women staff members.[7] Strangely enough, although somewhat less dramatically, the girls also appear to improve more rapidly.

The fact is that some children, particularly the male students, find it much easier to relate to a man and still retain their feelings of self-consistency with respect to maleness. It is not suggested that the female staff be replaced with all male faculties. If this were done, the subordinate roles of the sexes would simply be reversed. Rather, it is suggested that provisions should be made for a balancing of sex models. As was mentioned previously, Preston found the reverse circumstance common in the predominately male environments of the German schools.[8] Establishing models for both sexes, then, is the key to the proper treatment of this phase of curriculum development.

The process of including models for the sexes in the curriculum is not especially difficult. However, some caution must be used in the selection of these models. As has been known for some time, girls do not relate easily to women with manly voices and habits. Similarly, boys do not find it easy to develop close relationships with prissy, feminine men teachers. Children want their teachers or models to play the roles which society prescribes for their respective sexes. Boys like men who are manly; girls like women to be feminine. Moreover, boys find it easier to relate to women who are consistent with their female position and girls want men to be men. Caution should be used, then, in the selection of models in the instructional program.

Developing curriculum which will be mindful of the sexes in the classroom must be viewed in the light of all elements which will be included in the learning environment. Instructional materials and programs must be developed in such a manner as to recognize fully the male interests of boys, and those girls who may have similar interests, and, at the same time, make provisions for the leaders with respect to both sexes. In this manner, sex consideration is given to the total environment as organized.

[7] William Doolittle, "Teacher Plays 'Big Daddy' Successfully in Newark," *Education*, Vol. 3, (September, 1968) p. 9.

[8] Ralph C. Preston, "Reading Achievement of German and American Children," *School and Society*, Vol. 90.

Specific suggestions for a masculine curriculum and male models

The following suggestions are given only with the intent of demonstrating fully the fundamental elements which may be made a part of a sex-considerate curriculum. Upon these suggestions, or other similar factors, can be established an instructional program that will have built-in attractions for male students.

Male models

1. *Men teachers in all levels of the school program.*

> This is an ideal solution to this curriculum provision. Unfortunately, attracting male teachers has long been recognized as a problem at all levels of the elementary school program. Getting them into the primary grades is even more difficult. The restrictions, although imaginary in most instances, need to be clearly removed, however, in order that men may feel they have a place in the primary grades.
>
> If it is possible to retain men for the teaching positions in the primary grades, it would be advisable to develop cooperative relationships between the male and female teachers at this level in order to avoid the obvious faults of male or female dominance.

2. *Male teachers' aides assigned to female teachers for continuous classroom assistance.*

> This form of instructional leadership has become more and more common with the growth of programs specifically designed for educationally handicapped instructional programs. The utilization of teachers' aides, and particularly the use of male aides, has had tremendously valuable effect upon the effectiveness of the instructional leadership. It might be added, that prior

educational training for teachers' aides is not particularly important. Aides lacking professional education may be given such training subsequent to their employment. They are able to begin with a commitment to children and little education and grow into the responsibilities in an in-service education program. Limited orientation for both professional educators and teachers' aides is all that is necessary prior to implementation of such a program.

3. *Male counselors may be employed and utilized to assist in provisions for male models in the elementary school.*

Attention has been given for some time to the need for guidance and counseling in the elementary school. Such counseling is most desirable at an age when it can be most effective. The employment of male counselors with full access to the classrooms of the school will give the boys a constant male model. This will be of particular importance if the teachers will utilize this person in the planning and implementation of instructional programs.

4. *Male resource visitors may be brought into the implementation of the curriculum.*

Utilizing a regularly prescribed list of men from the community as resource persons can be the least expensive and most practical of the methods for bringing masculinity into the classroom. Such resource persons may be fathers and older relatives of the students. However, it is more desirable to develop contacts from the community at large. These men may be industrialists, employees of local government agencies, men with hobbies or experiences appropriate to the instructional program, or simply men with a desire to take part in the classroom program. If a sufficiently large list of "regulars" is developed, none will find the requests for their time a burden. However, each should be considered for more than one visitation and for out-of-school contact in a prescribed manner by students in the class.

The selection of community male models should be appropriate to the identified interests which are common to most boys. That is, men with substantial knowledge of outdoor interests, action vocations, and extensive experiences in exploration of particular fields, will be more effective with children. In the process of making selections of male community resources, the teacher should personally interview each in order to avoid the pitfalls of selecting men with the desired knowledge, but without the qualities which make for effective presentations to children.

5. *Male tutors may be utilized as a part of the regular instructional program of the school.*

The opportunity for older boys to serve in brief periods of the instructional schedule as tutors for students in the primary grades is available in nearly every school. Such "tutors" may assist the teachers as guides on field trips, in classroom activities, or on the playground. Each such tutor must be carefully instructed as to the type of responsibilities which he can assume, but the freedom of activity which permits close relationships with individual students is desirable. The utilization of older boys as tutors must be organized in such a manner as to provide male models over a reasonable period of time. Too frequent changes in the tutors will not permit students to identify closely with them. However, the schedules for the utilization of older students in this role should be considerate of their own study program.

The reader can easily expand upon this list of male models in a manner most appropriate to his program. It is necessary at this point to make suggestions with respect to the other factors in the curriculum which will assist in giving the instructional program an orientation responsive to male interests. Again, this listing is only suggestive and may be easily expanded by the teacher in accord with his specific program.

Male curriculum elements

1. *Activity centers*, sometimes referred to as learning centers, may be established in any of the classrooms of the elementary school. Such centers must be considerate of the vast differences in male interests—and in female interests—and fully a part of the regular classroom environment. These centers may include at least the following topical orientations:

a. *Science centers* with appropriate equipment and materials for active exploration.

b. *Construction centers*, with appropriate manuals, plans, and diagrammatic materials permitting freedom of individual action without additional direction. Such centers would, of course, necessitate the provisions for constrution materials and tools to be utilized.

c. *Art media centers* with all of the fundamental varieties of materials and equipment. Clay with boards and modeling tools, paints, brushes, paper, and easels, materials for collage, yarns, cloth, colored chalk, pencils, felt pens, and all the materials that are appropriate should be included in this center.

d. *Writing centers* should be established to permit the students to utilize this media of expression in much the same manner as they would utilize the media mentioned above. The writing center may include pens, pencils, felt pens (which boys thoroughly enjoy), paper, binding materials for booklets, staples, glue, idea boxes for inspiration, pictures for similar use, dictionaries, and simple directions for acceptable formats (a wide variety) of written products.

e. *Library and reading centers* with sufficient variety in the materials provided to recognize the interests of all students. Such a center might include books, magazines, other children's written stories, records, tape recordings of stories, filmstrips with individual viewers, and picture collections, either bound or unbound. Frequent changes in the materials of this center are important, perhaps more important than in the other centers. Moreover, children should not feel that they must "check out" materials they wish to use.

2. *Study trips* also provide an essential element in the instructional program. These trips are easily oriented to include the special interests of boys as well as girls. Rather than identify particular types of visitations which may be made outside of the classroom, as these will vary to a large extent in each community, it is more appropriate here to indicate the orientation of such field studies. Consideration should be given to each of the following elements with respect to study trips.

a. *Selection of places for visitation* which relate to both the male and female functions in society. For example, a visitation to a department store may be appropriate if the students visit departments of the store which are frequented by both men and women. Missing the hardware department in favor of a visitation to the clothing department would give such a visitation a feminine slant and would be unfortunate.

b. *Selection of contact persons* at the place of visitation in order to capitalize upon male models would be important to consideration of male interests.

c. *Utilization of both male and female assistant teachers* and older students in the supervision of the children on a field study would lend much to the success of the trip.

d. *Integrating the findings and experiences* of the field trip into the fundamental classroom program in such a manner as to permit the boys to see the male functions of the study. This may well mean calling attention to the male factors of the visitation center.

e. *Providing for the variety of methods* which children may wish to utilize in expressing their reactions and learnings as a result of a study trip. Boys may prefer to use the art center or a tape recording rather than the more feminine composition which is frequently the asked-for expression.

It would be wrong to close this chapter on the discussion of curriculum and male models without briefly calling attention to the atmosphere of the classroom, which can be given either a male or a female orientation. In this discussion, attention is called to the elements of the classroom which would not include the printed materials of the curriculum or the male models used for instructional leadership.

The very manner in which the teacher organizes a classroom may make it inviting or offensive to boys. Although these are elements not normally considered as a part of the curriculum, they are features of the learning environment and, therefore, can properly be considered in this chapter.

If the teacher organizes all materials in a strict, neat, and most precise manner, boys will tend not to function well with these materials. In fact, it is just possible that the girls will not either. Cleanliness is important to all children, but precise order is not. Children can be viewed much in the same light as women at a store sale. If the items are dumped upon a table, somehow they become far more attractive. Much the same psychology can be applied to students, particularly boys.

Teachers must allow for "messing around" in the processes of exploration. Although this is not an orderly process, the degrees of student participation in such an environment are infinitely greater than they are in a precisely structured setting.

The organization of tables, desks, bulletin boards, shelves, work spaces, and cupboards must be such as to encourage the free exploration by the students in the classroom. Although this may not be as pleasing to the ordered character of the teacher, or, more particularly, the wishes of the custodian or principal, children will function at a much more effective level in such an environment.

Recalling, then, the many facets of this chapter, the reader will recognize that all individuals and elements included in a classroom laboratory should be considered as the curriculum. Each element should be related to male interests.

REFERENCES

Association for Supervision and Curriculum Development, *New Insights and the Curriculum*, Alexander Frazier, Editor and Chairman, 1963 Yearbook Committee, Washington, D.C.: A.S.C.D., 1963.

Doolittle, William, "Teacher Plays 'Big Daddy' Successfully in Newark," *Education*, 3: 9, September 1968.

Fader, Daniel N., and McNeil, Elton B. *Hooked on Books*, Berkeley, California: Berkeley Publishing Corp., 1968.

Kostick, M. M., "A Study of Transfer: Sex Differences in the 'Reasoning Process'," *Journal of Educational Psychology*, 45: 449–458, December 1954.

Sears, Robert R., Maccoby, Eleanor E., and Levin, Harry, *Patterns of Child Rearing*, Evanston, Ill.: Row Peterson and Co., 1967.

Warner, Sylvia Ashton, *Teacher*, New York: Simon and Schuster Inc., 1963.

chapter six

Programs of instruction considerate of sex differences

The processes of restructuring programs of instruction with particular focus upon sex differences and with full cognizance of the
different learning modes for boys and girls, must include an awareness
of the previously stated comments concerning self-perception. It will
be recalled that a student's progress is determined by his ability to
interact with his environment. If the male student cannot accept an
active, participatory role in what is an essentially feminine mode of
instruction because of perceptions he has of himself and the over-
whelming desire to remain consistent with these perceptions, then the
programs of instruction will not be effective.

It is not enough to include male models in the learning setting
or to couple with such models curriculum that permits a male focus,
although these factors are essential to the larger provisions for the
male in the school setting. With these factors must be joined a method
of instruction that also allow boys the opportunities to participate as
boys, thus maintaining the essentials of self-consistency.

Adjusting instructional methods to allow full consideration of the
individual students and their particular modes of learning is more
complex than reorienting the curriculum. Because of the influences of

the home and studies in previous grade levels, the distinctions between the methods of learning utilized by the sexes, or just by individual students within a sex group, are less clearly defined. Moreover, the methods utilized by the students will vary frequently, even within a subject. Therefore, it may be necessary for the teacher to discard one learning theory in favor of another.

If the educational system has generally been developed in accord with the association theories of learning, as is most frequently the case, teaching techniques and instructional media will be highly formalized and predicated upon attention to the group rather than the individual. For the general instructional program, such a structure will need to be radically altered if it is to be adequate for individual students. Conversely, if the foundation of the educational system is built upon the field theories of learning, much will already have been done to provide for the individual student.[1] It is necessary, then, for the prospective teacher to determine the learning theory or theories which seem most appropriate and become sufficiently conversant with their techniques to be comfortable in their use.

A presentation of the full range of learning theories would not be appropriate here. Such a study is complex and would require more space than can be provided in this chapter. However, certain essential differences in the extremes of the continuum for learning theories will be treated here in order that the reader may make gross discriminations required to implement the tenets of this program.

Although it is somewhat unfair to the authors of the varied learning theories to place each of these learning philosophies upon a single continuum, such a procedure will readily illustrate the fundamental variations and conflicting elements to be found in each of the theory groups. The continuum below contains in imprecise and overlapping form many theories and modifications of theories. Therefore, it is only in the extremes of the continuum that precise distinctions become clearly identified. The presentation in this chapter will be in terms of the extremes of this continuum.

association theories	field theories
(group attention)	(individual attention)

[1] Morris L. Bigge, *Learning Theories for Teachers*, New York, Harper & Row, Publishers, 1964.

The parenthesized labels are presented to generally identify the major teaching stress placed upon each of the extremes in this illustration of learning theories.

Each group of learning theories, when compared with the alternate group at the other end of the continuum, has characteristics which will assist in the interpretation of each. The listing of the characteristics of each group is intended to be no more than just enough to illustrate the major distinctions.

Association theories of learning might best be characterized as having the following traits in greater or lesser amounts in accord with their placement upon the continuum, either toward the extreme or toward the middle.

1. *A study of parts.*

   In this respect consideration of the body of material to be learned is broken into smaller parts for easy assimilation.

2. *A directed form of study.*

   The teacher directs the learning activities of the classroom in an obvious manner. With respect to this characteristic, it should be understood that the processes of teacher assignments, recitations, and testing are commonly utilized.

3. *Frequent repetitive exercises.*

   Drill, purposeful practice, and other similar terms would be characteristic of association theories of learning. It is understood that the greater the number of repetitions, the greater the learning.

4. *Stress by sequential learnings.*

   Presentations of concepts and learnings are necessarily ordered in a formal sequence to be observed by each student. Grade levels, textbooks, and programmed learnings would be consistent in this theory group.

Relating association theories to language development is relatively easy, inasmuch as the traditional format of instruction for this broad field of learning is commonly founded upon these theories.

Treated individually in the sequence of presentation, each of the traits would be interpreted in the language arts field in the following manner. With regard to the *study of parts*, the teacher would present the subdivisions of spelling, writing, speaking, and reading as separate parts within the broad language field. Moreover, each of the part, would be redivided into smaller learnings. For example, in writings each letter form would be presented independently from other letters of the alphabet, the assumption being that when each individual letter is learned, appropriate letters may be combined to make words which the child may write.

Assignments are presented in a *directed form* from teacher to student. It is accepted in this theory group that the teacher knows best which learning in language study should follow another learning. Such direction may follow a carefully prescribed sequence of lessons presented in a textbook, but determined by the teacher. Should a student wish to vary this selection of learnings, he would necessarily be in conflict with the directions being determined by the teacher. Learning, then, is externally controlled by the teacher.

Drill and continuous practice exercises are fundamental to the implementation of association theories. Therefore, repeated spelling drill on a given word list would be a common practice. The writing of a given word or words, ten times, twenty times, or even more would insure the student's success in spelling according to this characteristic of the association theory group.

Closely ordered sequences for the individual learnings of the separate studies in language would be consistent with association theories. The supposition is that the stories in the basal reading series are arranged in order of difficulty; in fact, the level of difficulty for the vocabulary is also ordered, beginning theoretically with the more easily learned words and proceeding to the more difficult words as the sequence is followed. Skipping about in the reading book is impossible for a child in this theory group. In order for the child to be successful with the story toward the back of the book, it is necessary for him to read each story preceding it.

Fundamentally, though, the association theories are *group oriented*. The assumption is made that children must follow the program as it is presented without particular attention to their individual interests or talents.

An examination of the other extreme on the learning theory continuum, that position held by the *field theories*, will present the opposing approach to learning. For clarity, however, a list of corresponding characteristics is presented below in the manner used in the description of association theories.

1. *A study of fields.*

   Field theorists insist that learning of elements can only take place in relationship to the other units in a broader field. Word analysis skills are presented in the context of total sentences, not as they would relate to an independent or isolated single word.

2. *A nondirected form of study.*

   According to this trait, learning is essentially a self-directed function. Students are free to select the courses of action which they feel will lead them to the learning desired.

3. *A nonrepeating form of learning.*

   This characteristic illustrates the concept of *learning experiences* which are singular in nature and are not repeated through extensive drill. The essential factor is the assumption that applications or utilization of single learnings will take place only when such learnings are found in new fields as elements and that they are then utilized to assist the student with understanding of some new concept. Drill and practice is not necessary.

4. *Stress is placed upon units of learning.*

   Field theorists believe that learning takes place in fields or environments and, although a matter of finding known elements and using them to interpret new fields, it is not necessarily sequential in nature. Learning takes place in accord with the individual student's motivation and within a structure that is uniquely his own.

The application of field theories to language studies is essentially a recent development. Although, in the days of the one-room country school, teachers made excellent blends of reading, writing, and speaking divisions of language studies, this was done as a matter of program scheduling convenience. With the advent of language experience methodology, field theories were given conscious application.

Preconceived divisions of spelling, writing, reading, and speaking in language studies were eliminated. It was understood that writing is a logical extension of speaking and reading, a matter of relating previously written materials to the moment. A study of each could not be properly divorced from the total field.

Coupling the comprehensive relationships of all elements of the broad field of language study with the self-directing feature of field theory substantially changes the approaches utilized in language learnings. Predetermined formats for reading, writing, and speaking cannot be used. Students need the kinds of experiences which will stimulate them, as individuals, to speak or want to write. From these personal interpretations of experiences the foundations are presented for language learnings.

Repetitious studies of word lists in spelling would not be utilized in a language experience method because learning takes place through applications or utilization of words in writing. A student will expand his written and spoken vocabulary and, subsequently, his reading vocabulary in accord with his desire to relate experiences. Internal motivation is fundamental to language development.

Subsequently learnings and previously structured steps in the language development ladder are not required in a field theory, language experience program. Although many resources in book form are important to this method, textbooks and rigidly constructed curricula are not.

Stress in the field theory approaches to language development is placed upon the individual student and not upon group activities. Because attention in this book is placed upon the learning functions of the individual and the opportunities provided for such activity, precise descriptions of instructional techniques and methodology will further illustrate application of field theory as a foundation for the language arts program. Concern is for the individual and particularly for the male student in the program.

Although it may appear redundant, stress in all instruction must be predicated upon respect for the individual as an individual student and not as a member of some structured group. Preparation of lessons in language, as in other areas of instruction, must then begin with careful study of the individual needs of the students in the class. In essence, lessons are prepared with each member of the class. Teachers will recognize that there will be frequent overlapping of preparations for several individuals for a given learning. However, it is the recognition of the needs of the separate students which determines the instruction, not the needs of the group. Particular attention must be given to the needs of the male student.

To institute an adequate program of preparation with the individual student, it is necessary for the teacher to be continuously aware of the learning status and motivational aims of each student. This will require frequent and personal contacts with each child. These contacts may take the form of teacher-pupil conferences structured upon a semiformal basis, or the contacts may be *opportunity encounters* founded upon a free and open rapport between the teacher and the children in the classroom. Some teachers may find that a combination of these techniques is essential to good communication. Much of the benefit derived from the cooperative planning developed between the teacher and the individual student will be dependent upon the care used in the annotations kept for each pupil. Also, one of the most prominent dangers to the individualized instructional program lies in the system of annotation. Teachers need to gather the information necessary to do the individualized preparations so important to advancing the level of learning opportunities for each child. At the same time care must be used to prevent falling into the errors of group assessment.

In the planning of lessons or activities, teachers must not establish one formal check list of "possible weaknesses." Such a list would simply be another form of a formal ladder of instruction. Common measurement instruments used for all students in the class are group devices, not considerate of the individual pupils.

Through the techniques of teacher-pupil conferencing, teachers will find frequent overlapping of interests among the students in the class and the natural groups which may be formulated relative to common needs among several children.

The amount of time which will be required for communication sessions between the teacher and each child may vary, but seldom will it be necessary to devote more than five to ten minutes to any one session. Brief, but frequent conferences are of far more value. Further, it is not necessary for the teacher to hold formal sessions with each child every day. That is not to say that the teacher should not find it necessary to talk with each pupil each day, however. This opportunity for each student to talk to the teacher every school day is fundamental to building and maintaining a strong rapport. Meetings for the purposes of assessment by students with their teacher are not necessary each day. In fact, many of the students will acquire the skills of independent action very quickly. These students will need fewer assessment conferences with the teacher.

To utilize fully the resources available for student planning, a free atmosphere must prevail in the classroom. If individual pupils have the opportunity to test their planning of activities or ideas upon other students in the classroom, much additional assistance can be provided. Students get much direction from other students. All of this frees the teacher to become available to others in the class. Moreover, it will be found that boys will test their thinking with other boys. The male interests will not be subjected to the critical assessment of female judgment. This can be extremely valuable to the provisions for adequate maleness in the program of instruction.

Planning of instructional programs in language arts must be cognizant of the fundamentally oral character of this field of study.[2] Opportunities for the formulation of individual studies in reading or other forms of language must begin with oral interpretations. Through these individual oral examinations or reflections upon topics, the teacher gains insights into the particular interests and understandings of each child. More importantly, male interpretations are presented. This will give the teacher much useful guidance in the preparations for learning activities considerate of sex differences among the individual pupils.

When planning learning activities, the teacher must make adequate provisions for varying levels of performance for the individual student. Each child will fluctuate between maximum learning efforts and moments of little devotion to his studies. This is particularly true for boys. Recognition of this generalization will preclude any formal grouping of students for extensive periods of time, because such groupings force the child to maintain one general level of performance. Freedom to delve deeply into a given study or to treat a subject lightly will encourage greater learning over a long period of time. Capitalizing upon periods of high interest in planning of learning activities,

[2] Robert B. Rudell, "The Effect of Oral and Written Patterns of Language Structure on Reading Comprehension," *The Reading Teacher*, Vol. XVIII, January, 1965 pp. 270–275.

then, becomes of vital importance in the consideration of programs for the individual.

Provisions for language study in the elementary schools should be such that the total field of language development is considered as an integral program without unique divisions. This understanding forces the elimination of the traditional "reading schools." Stress needs to be placed upon all phases of language study with more or less equal emphasis.

Periods set aside for the purpose of reading study separate from the writing studies will be eliminated. Spelling instruction, separate from and unrelated to other language studies, would be inconsistent with serious and intelligent planning for language instruction. As has been indicated previously, the fundamental importance of oral language to writing and writing to reading must be recognized. Individual instruction in particular skills must always be in relationship to the total field of language development. Also, the total field of language study must be consistent with the highly individualized interests of each student in the classroom. Moreover, for the effective development of oral language, provisions must be made for intelligent listening among the students. The study of listening skills becomes, then, a part of the total field of language study.

Beginning with the *oral foundation* for language and then proceeding to the writing and reading phases of the total field will give logic to the learnings. Spelling then finds itself as a functional element in the broader study of written language activity. Oral reading utilizes all of the other provisions of language instruction.

The simultaneous provisions for all elements of the broad language field, coupled with the particular interests of students, makes the total program of instruction far more rich and satisfying to the individual learner. Particularly important, though, each child can find himself in the total program of construction.

The instructional program for the language arts cannot be developed without serious consideration of all other phases of the elementary school curriculum. The utilization of language development in the fields of social studies, science, mathematics, music, art, and other studies gives practical application to language learnings. Further, the students, particularly the boys, find that they may pursue their topics in science and develop their language skills at the same time. Through this integration of studies in the elementary program each student has a substantially broader field in which to function and develop.

Preparations for a rich language learning program needs also to consider the tremendous value of first-hand experiences. Opportunities for exploration and discovery in laboratories cognizant of individual interests will heighten the excitement of learning. Emphasis should be upon actual rather than vicarious experiences, particularly in the primary grades. For boys, action-oriented experiences are of special importance and will substantially improve individual achievement in language learning.

Establishing opportunities for free exploration, full utilization of resources, action exploration, conversation, joint study, and freedom of movement in the classroom to facilitate self-directed studies will also increase the noise level within the room. Although such increased noise levels may be more unpleasant to the teacher, children are seldom disturbed by this. The student's toleration of motion and noise exceeds that of any adult. Moreover, superficial observations of these activities may indicate confusion in the classroom. If the motivation is high, however, for each student, there will not be confusion, but greater learning.

The teacher should also make a conscientious effort to remove all external pressures from the child. Time assignments, predetermined goals, and negative criticism of a student's efforts hinder his growth in language development. It is necessary that each child sees himself as important and successful. Plateaus of satisfying rest before reaching for a new goal must be available through each child's personal pacing of his study. It is noted, too, that teachers' expectations for performance levels for children are rarely accurate or consistent with the individual's abilities.

Individualizing opportunities for learning is a highly complex task for the teacher. Properly accomplished, however, the results can be almost phenomenal.

Specific tasks in preparing individualized language instruction

In the rest of this chapter, specific suggestions are provided to assist the teacher in directing his activities toward the individual students in a manner considerate of sex differences and motivating interests. Of course, these suggestions are given without particular consideration for achievement levels among students or their status in the program of elementary education. Therefore, each will have to be adapted to the level of instruction being provided and the setting which governs the program.

1. Determine the particular interests of each student in the class and the approximate range of reading ability.

2. Collect books, magazines, pictures, pamphlets, filmstrips, and other reading materials in quantities of at least 5 to 10 books or items per child in the class.

3. Design a plan, with appropriate variations suitable for each student, for holding individual conferences with pupils for assessing and recording abilities and needs, preparing specialized learning opportunities, discussing interests, and sharing each pupil's reading material.

4. Discuss the reading program with the class before individual selections of books or reading materials are made.

5. Make books and other reading materials easily available on tables or shelves. Particularly inviting to boys are random piles of books dumped upon a table.

6. Invite children to select freely one or more books of particular interest without restriction as to title or time of selection.

7. Show enthusiasm for reading and an interest in children's books by reading short passages aloud to individuals or to small groups.

8. If the teacher is male, it is of particular value to read aloud to the total class. Boys do not often see fathers read. If the teacher is female, she may read regularly to the total class to introduce varied topics and special books of general interest. However, it might be well for the woman teacher to invite the male principal to read to the class upon occasion as a stimulus to the boys' interests.

9. Help children share their books by meeting with small groups with common interests. This may mean meeting with the mystery book group, adventure book group, or some other popular interest group.

10. Encourage dramatization, reading aloud to others, rewriting of endings, preparing sequel stories with the same characters, or the preparation of art media interpretations of parts or particular actions within the story.

11. Prepare and make available collections of stories written by members of the class. These may be typed and bound and circulated among the commercially published books and materials in the classroom, or added to the school library.

Each of the suggestions provided in the foregoing list can be expanded and modified in accord with the individual talents of the classroom teacher and in consideration of the activities of special interest to students in a class.

The teacher may, however, make other preparations which will stimulate activity and study in the broad field of language. A random selection of such tasks is presented in the following list. Each activity may relate to one or more phases or elements of the total instructional program in language or, in fact, to any of the many facets of the total curriculum for the elementary school.

1. Establish learning centers in the interest areas and permit free exploration relative to particular interests. This provision may lead to the development of laboratories in various parts of the room to which individuals or small groups may go for free exploration.

2. Make provision for frequent excursions for first-hand experiences outside the classroom to be followed by active and open discussions by the students relative to their experiences.

3. Prepare picture collections, title card files, beginning paragraph cards, situational description files, and other similar stimulating resources which will encourage children to write, read, or want to speak about some new topic.

4. Tape stories without endings to be replayed at the listening center by students as a stimulus to their writing.

5. Provide opportunities for children to have many sensory experiences.

6. Encourage children to talk about their experiences and express their feelings and ideas in speech, art media, body movements, or writing.

7. Record children's expressions and stories exactly as they are composed and dictated by the child-authors.

8. Encourage the authors to copy these dictated stories and read them aloud to teachers' aides, other children, and visitors to the classroom.

9. As young authors become more proficient in handwriting, encourage them to write independently.

10. Type original stories, bind them into books to be catalogued and circulated through the school library.

11. Place the bound copies of children's stories upon the reading table to be circulated within the room to other children.

12. Provide resources for spelling and vocabulary development. These may take the form of teacher-prepared lists with additional words being added by the students as new words are encountered.

13. Establish experimentation centers which will give opportunities for free exchange of ideas and, in turn, increase the arts of conversation and discussion, especially among boys.

Individualized programs require the teacher to function as a provider of resources. Collecting, changing, and mounting of pictures, setting up laboratories, finding new and stimulating topics, resource persons and materials, capitalizing upon student resources, and a multitude of other tasks require the enthusiasm and resourcefulness of the teacher. All of this is strenuous, but will provide highly satisfying results.

Implications for the instructional program

1. What are the specific handicaps imposed upon the boy when he is subjected to the application of an association theory of learning?

In the very direct sense, boys will not be subjected to an application of any theory of learning. Learning theories are not applied in the same sense as assignments in subject matter or, for that matter, the curriculum in mathematics. Learning theories are carefully formulated theories which serve to guide the formulation of total learning programs and the procedures to be utilized within these programs. Assuming, however, that an association theory has been used to structure the language program in which the student is to function, then this question can be answered directly. First, the boy will be handicapped in the sense that he has absolutely nothing to do with the selection of goals or the steps leading to these goals. Lack of participation in these activities certainly promotes disinterest in the total study field. Secondly, boys functioning in a program guided by association theories normally are externally directed in their learning activities. They are asked to respond in accord with directions given either by the teacher or by printed statements in the textbook. The program is established in advance without particular concern for the individual student's interests or desires. In this form, the student is asked to respond in at least semi-robot fashion to prescribed activity steps presented. The feeling of personal involvement is not required and therefore the student is frequently handicapped by a constant feeling of detachment from the whole learning function. Thirdly, association theories assume a fundamental place for repetitive activities. The more drill, the more firmly a concept is founded in the boy's mind and, hence, the greater the learning which is supposedly taking place. The fact that the boy grasps the concept on the first activity is not important. Repetition is still expected. The monotony of such a program is especially devastating to the desires for learning among boys who enjoy exploration and discovery. Imagine the feeling of depression which settles upon a boy when he opens the text for language in September and can see what he is to do throughout the entire school term. This is a factor of the application of an association theory of learning.

2. *Why is it necessary for the teacher to be continuously aware of the learning status and motivational aims of each student?*

In a program which is truly considerate of individual differences and in a plan which does not impose total structures for learning upon students, the role is different for the teacher than it would be in a program with a group orientation. A teacher functioning in an individualized, nondirective classroom assumes the major role of being a resource to learning in the classroom. This is quite different from being the total, directive source in that teachers must function in response to students' needs. To accomplish the role as a resource to learning, the teacher must be continuously aware of the current status of each student. Only in this manner can she know what materials and other resources she will need to make available to the student. Moreover, knowing the precise needs of students allows the teacher to know the most opportune moments for giving instruction in skills which will be directly applicable to studies. There are, of course, many other reasons which insist that a teacher knows the relative positions of students in their learning programs. In summary, it can be said that such knowledge is important if the teacher is to be helpful to boys.

REFERENCES

Allen, Roach Van, and Allen, Claryce, *Language Experiences in Reading, Level I*, Chicago: Encyclopedia Britannica Press, 1966.

────── *Language Experiences in Reading, Level II*, Chicago: Encyclopedia Britannica Press, 1966.

────── *Language Experiences in Reading, Level III*, Chicago: Encyclopedia Britannica Press, 1967.

────── *Language Experiences in Reading, Level III*, Chicago: Encyclopedia Britannica Press, 1967.

Bigge, Morris L., *Learning Theories for Teachers*, New York: Harper and Row, Publishers, 1964.

Holt, John, *How Children Learn*, New York: Pitman Publishing Corporation, 1967.

Lee, Doris May, and Allen, Roach Van, *Learning to Read Through Experience*, New York: Appleton-Century-Crofts, 1963.

Nichols, Ralph, and Lewis, Thomas R., *Listening and Speaking*, Dubuque, Iowa: W. C. Brown, 1954.

Veatch, Jeannette, *Individualizing Your Reading Program*, New York: Putnam, 1959.

Chapter seven

Continuous assessment techniques considerate of sex differences

Improving the total educational program in a manner which provides vastly increased opportunities for the male students requires a plan for continuous evaluation. Assuming a wholly valid process of assessment—one that is consistent with the philosophical aims of the program—each evaluation will serve to further improve the learning prospects for boys. Indeed, the wise coupling of assessment techniques with curriculum planning and the formulation of instructional methodology will support the continued improvement of learning opportunities for all students.

It is of fundamental importance that the system of measurement being used in the schools be in philosophical accord with the learning theory being implemented. Assessing students' educational placement and learning functions with a limited, feminine set of instruments while implementing instructional programs cognizant of distinct differences between the sexes cannot help but produce false findings. Such a process could be compared to measuring the products of the Ford Motor Company with aviation instruments. The aims of the two are simply not comparable.

The abilities of boys to function within the broad spectrum of male educational opportunities provided by an adjusted curriculum and instructional methodology must be measured in the light of these opportunities. To properly redirect educational programs in a manner considerate of masculine interests forces one to discard techniques of assessment which are either feminine in structure or formulated upon a basis which prevents sex orientation. Most nationally distributed standardized instruments are formed in a manner to prevent giving an advantage to either sex. Such instruments would have limited usefulness in a program considerate of the behavior of either sex group. This can also be said of teacher-made assessment instruments developed prior to varying the curriculum to include boys

In summary, it can be said that assessment techniques and instruments must be consistent with the educational opportunities available to children. Moreover, the program of assessment cannot include devices developed in a "sexless" or group-oriented instructional program.

Another point of critical importance, and one which will be given more space in Chapter 8, is the interpretation of societal measurements of the educational system. These assessments, either directly or indirectly, have much to do with the product assessment of the school system. Traditional measures used by society to review the programs of the schools are generally good and important in keeping the schools in step with society's interpretations of their functions.

In some fundamental respects, however, the wants of the public are simply not consistent with what educators know to be the needs of society. For example, the belief that the ability to do rapid arithmetical computations indicates superior educational achievement simply is not correct. Moreover, such a belief is really not consistent with the functional demands of a modern nation. This is a skill given over to machines in the present age. Society also expects all students to have certain common educational experiences. This may be well and good. However, when such experiences are noted by the public, high among the learnings listed are the traditional subjects of the school: English, Mathematics and the Sciences. Far down the list would be found the integral functions of the social sciences. Further down would be found art, music, literature, and other humanities. Educators know such a list to be quite out of harmony with the sociological needs of a culture.

It is important that the schools be responsive to the wishes of society. Such responsiveness does not mean, however, that educators should be directed by society in such a manner as to ignore the leadership role for which they are employed. An over-response can be observed in the "industrial" structure employed for assessment in the educational system by a majority of the nation's schools.

Much as industry has developed a system of precise measurement for production, schools have attempted to implement micro-measurement of the learning product. Although uniformity may be a remarkable attribute of a manufactured product, it is not to be desired in the educational system.

Uniform industrial measurements are common to group learning theories and the traditional "sexless" schools. Scarcely a school does not use standardized, uniform evaluation practices. These can be seen in a listing such as that noted below:

> uniform graduation or annual promotions.
> uniform grading systems.
> uniform minimum requirements.
> uniform behavioral patterns.
> uniform or singular curricular programs.
> uniform testing instruments.
> uniform time schedules for learning.

Such a listing could go on and on. The pattern would not be altered, however, and it is enough to look at this list and know that all of these practices are regimenting in nature and highly inconsistent with the individuality of the American democratic philosophy. In the sincere desire to fit the products of the nation's schools into society, conformity has been stressed to the detriment of the creativity which is critical to the dynamic character of the country. In this sense educators have injured the learning processes.

As a group, boys have been hurt the most in the present system because they do not view the school as being male oriented. To conform to the system means losing much of the maleness which is so important to them.

Before systems of assessment are presented which are consistent with self-directed and individualized programs of instruction, an acceptance of the following generalization should be achieved. The philosophy, curriculum, instructional methodology, and assessment techniques must be in full accord with one another. In school programs considerate of male learning abilities, each of these fundamentals must find a full place for boys.

Specific assessment techniques

In a society which places primary stress upon the rights and responsibilities of individuals, the educational program must be developed
upon these concepts. If the goal in society, and subsequently, the
educational system, is to increase the individual's functional abilities
with respect to himself and the greater good of society, then it is only
logical that fundamental assessments of the educational program be
viewed in the light of the individual.

Moreover, if self-direction is the key to the success of a democratic society, then it is also logical and proper that self-assessment be
the fundamental tool of measurement for use in the school. Such an
approach to assessment is consistent with the philosophical foundations of the educational system, the curriculum developed, and the
manner in which the program is implemented, if these programs are
considerate of the individual.

Self-directed assessment should be highly personalized. Moreover,
these personalized devices for measurement of success and failure
should not be restricted to the products constructed by the individual
student. The paper performances or oral presentations of the individual are only symptomatic or indicative of the fundamental changes
or lack of changes which are sought. Measurement then should be
viewed in the light of inner change which takes place with the individual student. Behavioral functions indicative of learnings, attitudinal change demonstrating broader viewpoints or refinements of
learnings are undoubtedly of greater importance to the total question
of assessment. The critical factors, though, are those elements which
the student deems to be important measures of his progress.

For a student to be able to assess adequately his progress it is
necessary for him to have a thorough understanding of his goals. The
student establishes these understandings through the implementation
of adequate teacher-pupil planning at the inception of particular
studies. These goals are kept clear in the student's mind throughout
the learning process by frequent teacher-student conferences. At these
times, each pupil is able to determine where he is with respect to the
end products which he has in mind.

Teachers assist individual pupils in their evaluations through a
variety of techniques, none of which imposes a format for assessment
upon the student. The teacher's techniques are centered around the

questions needed to assist the student in recognizing what he has been able to accomplish and those areas of study in which he has not devoted sufficient effort. Frequently, questions by the teacher will be used to call attention to facets of a learning field which the student has not clearly identified. The degree to which teachers are able to use specific questions relative to the student's study will be the degree to which the teacher is fully cognizant of what the student has been doing. Also, the implementing of specific questions in evaluation sessions clearly indicates the instructor's sincere interest in each student and his work. General questions, such as "What have you been doing in reading?" or "What did you like best about your studies?" give students the impression that the teacher has not been observant or that the only time when such work is important to the teacher is at the evaluation period. Carefully motivated studies which have been of particular benefit to students can be negated if the teacher is not just as careful with evaluations as he was with the motivating preparations.

In order that the teacher may ask appropriate questions of each student during the moments of evaluation, it is necessary for the instructor to be continuously aware of each pupil's efforts in the classroom. This will require keeping notations about the books a child is reading, the materials he has utilized, and the procedures he has been following. It may also require the teacher to read some of the same books, review the materials the student has used, and test the functions of apparatus or procedures the pupil included in his studies. Individual students also enjoy the give-and-take of sessions in which they can share their findings and have the teacher share his discoveries, even though these may be quite different. Much dignified discussion grows out of such reciprocal sessions.

Teachers must, then, prepare for evaluation sessions with individual pupils much as they would prepare the stimulating questions and presentations used to initiate a series of learnings for each student.

The formulation of questions and points for discussion with individual students need not be extensive. Neither is it necessary for evaluation sessions to be lengthy. The primary objective of such sessions should be to assist the student to determine areas needing further attention. When a student has recognized the limitations of his study, through the combined efforts of the teacher and himself, courses of action can be developed to initiate further study. All this is followed by the teacher's efforts to supply the needed resources, specialized assistance, and additional motivation for the student to continue.

It is important that the teacher avoid concluding evaluation interviews with a student by using artificial notations indicating some extrinsic or group mark for success. Grade marks, even though these may be as informal as a commonly used set of terms such as "good," "excellent," "fair," or "You can do better," are detrimental. If such terms are used for all of the students in the class, these words then become group measures of success and, in turn, do much to destroy the individualized program. Students are especially alert to the comments the teacher makes with respect to another student's achievement.

Evaluation goals, which are of real importance to the teacher, are all relative to understandings which the student acquires. In a sense, these are value changes made by students. A few examples are given below to demonstrate the types of value changes which indicate the fundamental achievements desired:

1. The student gains respect for his learning abilities and desires to continue his efforts.

2. The student acquires sufficient confidence in his abilities to permit his work to be scrutinized by others without fear or threat to his self-concept.

3. The student is able to see his work as having relevance to his personal wellbeing and feelings of individual worth.

4. The student is able to demonstrate a willingness to utilize newly acquired skills and learnings in applications to further studies.

5. The student is able to utilize the skills of self-criticism in ways which permit him to improve his learning efforts, giving recognition to his own particular talents and needs for improvement.

It will be noted that each of the values listed in the foregoing samples is indicative of inner change having basic significance to the total process of self-directed learning. These achievements will insure continued learning by each student with or without external assistance. None of these examples are externally imposed; nor do they have group value. Each is relative only to the pupil's feelings about himself in the environment of the school.

How, then, is it possible for the teacher to get the total process of individual assessment down to the specific identification of learning needs which will further the individual student's studies? If care is not used in this process, individual student identification of needs, and thus self-direction, is lost. The primary consideration is in the point of origin for needs for specific assistance in learning. *All identification of areas of weakness must begin with the student.*

Characteristically, in the traditional school program, group diagnostic techniques have been utilized. After the application of such examinations, the teacher prescribed particular instructional activities for those groups of students needing additional help. Some were motivated to apply themselves to these studies, but for the majority, the timing was wrong and the relative damage to the individual ego made these learning activities more painful than pleasant. Such devices would not be utilized in an individualized program. Rather, the teacher would establish the type of functional rapport with each student which would permit open conversation and discussion of his learning activities. In this process the student expresses his relative successes and identifies the areas of study which are giving him particular difficulty. At this stage, then, it is acceptable for the teacher to indicate that others are in need of similar assistance. A natural grouping can be formed about these specific needs identified by individuals and the instruction can be given. Using this generalized concept of assessment, the teacher is not trapped into imposing externally conceived devices which will threaten the individual. Moreover, the closeness of his working relationship with the individual students allows him the understanding necessary for nonthreatening group instruction. This latter is of particular importance for male students. Boys frequently will perform more successfully and with considerably greater confidence when the groups for specific learnings include only boys.

Originating the specific needs for particular instruction with identification by the individual students has significant value other than protection of the self-concept of each pupil. Such a process of assessment insures the relevance of the specialized instruction to learning difficulties which actually exist. Unnatural grouping of students for generalized presentations by the teacher is, at least, inefficient. Some students need instruction prior to the presentation. Other students have not identified the particular instruction as a need at the time when it is given. Only for a few will the teacher's presentation be timely. Moreover, to artificially group children for specific lessons may be disruptive to their individual programs of study at a time when their motivation is highest.

So traditional has the system of comparative grading and evaluation become in most schools that it is difficult for most teachers to ignore these processes completely. If, however, the teacher understands fully the fundamental premises upon which individualized instruction is based, he will be able to accept the elimination of group comparisons. The classroom application of comparative student measurements should not be used.

In many school districts, standardized measures are required of all teachers. School administrators and boards of education utilize these instruments to demonstrate the relative effectiveness of the programs which they supervise. Such applications are not necessarily harmful if the standardized tests are fully cognizant of sex differences and the programs of instruction. Often, however, this is not the case. Standardized instruments can be utilized by administrators if instructional programs are not formulated upon their results. Unfortunately, most nationally distributed tests of achievement are formulated in accord with traditional school programs. These programs are not considerate of individuals and consequently place boys at a serious disadvantage because they are not relevant to individually formulated programs of learning.

It should be clearly understood that standardized tests for achievement are *not* diagnostic examinations. The findings of such tests cannot be used intelligently to structure programs of instruction for individual students.

Another danger built into the application of standardized achievement tests, and one that is particularly damaging to the male student, is related to the methods utilized to standardized examinations are, at least in theory, sexless in their orientation. In this sense, the tests purport to give advantage to neither the girls nor the boys, but rather treat them equally. With respect to the item construction for these instruments, generally the sexless characteristic is accurate. In the determination of "norms" or "medians," however, these tests have a specific advantage for the girls.

Great care is taken in the standardization of an achievement test for national distribution. In this process, special care is used to permit a full range of responses, and in this manner, allow the students to obtain the best possible placement with respect to their learning levels. If such examinations are relative to the curriculum of the schools, however, and if these examinations consider the instructional methods most commonly employed in the nation's schools, then it follows that these examinations place male students at a serious disadvantage. The curricula of the schools and the instructional techniques are, as has been established, clearly feminine. Girls, by reason of the existing common structure, have the advantage. Boys can be expected to place lower as a group than do girls and they do, with marked consistency. These tests serve to provide further evidence to the boys that they are inferior students. All of this only compounds the problems already built into the structure of our feminine educational system.

Much of the pressure placed upon the educational system to provide statistical evidence in support of existing programs comes from the very programs of instruction which are built into the structure. More, however, comes as a result of the commonly used teaching methods.

Educators frequently justify the examination and grading systems by saying that the public demands such data. In addition, those school districts studying the problem of testing and grading students, and subsequently, altering the system to one that is less formal and more informative, have all too frequently returned to the "old" system because parents demanded this of them. Such justification is not honest, though, and certainly does not reflect intelligent professional leadership.

First, it should be reiterated that the philosophy of the school, the curriculum, the teaching methodology, and the evaluation system are profoundly interrelated. Educators cannot rightfully change one factor without changes in all other elements of the school program. Knowing this, educators must recognize the need to update all elements of philosophy, curriculum, instructional techniques, and evaluation simultaneously.

A second factor, an important recognition for educators, is that the public and particularly the parents of the children in the system, have a right to know, in as much detail as is possible, the status and activities of the school program. Under traditional circumstances and in lieu of an intelligible presentation of programs relative to the activities of the school system, the public has accepted test scores and a letter marking method. Some have discovered that these communiques don't tell a parent much. In fact, serious study of report cards and achievement test scores leads to discoveries that cannot help but be disturbing.

The real activities of children in a learning situation cannot be equated with letter grades or single test scores. Moreover, such scores do not provide the public with indicators of motivation or retention of information. Each is only a momentary measure, subject to all of the environmental and emotional stresses of the moment of record. In addition, such marks are relative to interpretations of the student's standing in a group. This group may be his class at school, or the standardization group used to structure a nationally distributed test. In short, such scores are delivered in the light of highly competitive circumstances. They really do not tell anything about what the student is able to accomplish in concert with his abilities and motivation although this is the information which parents really want. They do not know how to ask for it.

What is it, then, that schools must do to communicate to parents accurate information regarding their children's efforts in the school system? Coupling all factors of the educational system, as is necessary when reviewing the evaluation structure, changes in evaluation similar to the changes in philosophy, curriculum, and instructional methodology must be affected. If the philosophy, curriculum, and teaching strategies are firmly focused upon providing guidance and assistance to individual students in their studies and, if efforts in the organization of this educational system are aimed at highly motivated, self-directed learning environments for the students, then the formulation of reporting methods for parents must be along these same lines. *Evaluation must be a matter of self-assessment by each student. Reporting methods must be through the same channel.*

If students are highly motivated and openly excited about the activities of the school, parents will know of this. Also, in most instances, this student-reporting will be sufficient. Some children do not, however, have parents as interested in their activities as they should be. For this reason, teacher-student-parent conferences can easily be arranged to establish the circumstances of communication. Such conferences need not be "sit-down" affairs, but can be meetings at which time the student "walks the parent through" the resources he is using in the classroom and, with some questioning by the teacher, discusses his utilization of these materials or performance in each of the divisions of the learning laboratory. In such a manner, parents can be exposed to the individual facets of the program and receive interpretations of this learning setting in the light of their child's interests and assessments.

Teachers need to realize that students' methods of communicating with parents are predicated upon several factors. Some of these will be related to the parents' willingness to listen, of course. At least one approach to this problem has been discussed. However, other factors are involved. If the student is to report to his parents upon the activities in which he is functioning, then the pupil must be a true participant in a program of learning.

In the traditional educational program, in which the child is a recipient but not a participant, communication must be limited to reactions to teacher's presentations. If these interpretations are limited in the classroom, then the pupils' communiques to parents will be all the more restricted. When the organization of the educational laboratory is such that each student is functioning through motivation, self-direction and a process of self-assessment, each pupil will be able to discuss or demonstrate, in great detail, his part in the learning environment. In such an organization, the role of the individual pupil becomes prominent and comparisons with other students are sharply lessened.

Keys to evaluation are found not in a study of assessment techniques, but in the philosophy, curriculum, and teaching methodology employed in the formulation of the school programs. All must be consistent with one another.

REFERENCES

Charter, W. W., and Gage, N. L., *Readings in the Social Psychology of Education*, Boston: Allyn and Bacon Inc., 1963.

de Hirsch, Katrina, Jansky, Jeannette Jefferson, and Langford, William S., *Predicting Reading Failure*, New York: Harper and Row, Publishers, 1966.

Durkin, Dolores, *Children Who Read Early*, New York: Teachers' College Press, 1966.

Lyles, Thomas B., "Grouping by Sex," *The National Elementary Principal*, 46: 38–41, November 1966.

Stanchfield, Jo M., "Boys' Achievement in Beginning Reading," *Reading and Inquiry*, pp. 290–299, Proceedings of the Annual Convention, International Reading Association, Volume 10, Newark, Delaware, 1965.

chapter eight

Review of critical factors in a program of language development

Understanding the fundamentals of a newly formed program of instruction—in this instance, a program of language development which recognizes the need for a male learning environment—is essential to the careful planning of classroom learning opportunities. Conveying the need for such a program to the policy making body in an educational system and to the community is quite another function. This, too, is manifestly important to the realization of change in educational systems and provisions for new learning opportunities.

Educators, desiring to broaden the scope of programs of language and reading instruction to include stimulating activities related to the motivating interests of boys, must be capable of defining the limitations of the existing program. This must be coupled with the ability to define the elements of the newly formed structure with the necessary precision to permit lay governing boards and the community sufficient insight into the new program to allow for intelligent decisions regarding change. Being able, then, to outline the major concepts related to the development of a program for reading and language instruction which allows for full participation by male students in concise and understandable language is vitally important.

This chapter provides for a brief review of the major precepts of this book, permitting easy understanding of the needs for change in the reading and language learning opportunities in the schools. It is intended that a clear summary will be given of these fundamental understandings in a manner which allows for ease of communication of these ideas to lay governing boards and to parents and citizens of the community.

The feminine character of american education

An examination of the discriminating features of the American school system leaves little doubt that a conflict exists between dual standards of society for the sexes and the single, feminine nature of the public schools.

Societal expectations

Society expects boys to function in accord with precise male codes through the dictation of standards of conduct. These male standards encourage, at least to some major degree, the traits of individuality, including courage, curiosity, robustness, vigorous activity, and other similar characteristics. These are the precise elements of the male character which are not provided for, indeed not allowed, in the traditional school setting.

The more feminine traits of neatness, orderliness, obedience, and studiousness are the expectations of the school environment. The attempts to enforce these standards upon boys in the school program place the boys at a serious disadvantage. Their learning opportunities are severely handicapped.

The unquestioned, single standard

So traditional to the format of the school program has been the single feminine standard that many educators and, indeed, most lay citizens have accepted the tenent that boys are naturally slower to learn and that they perform less well in language development programs. It is assumed that girls possess a stronger verbal character than do boys. The fact that only a feminine program is offered seems not to have been considered as a handicap to the boys. A general acceptance of these notions results in the formulation of programs which accentuate the problems of the male students.

The format of instruction has been rigidly structured along group, female lines. Little allowance has been made for the individuality of learning opportunities in the materials or modes of instruction. The unquestioned acceptance of such a format provides a false premise upon which total programs have been developed. Although attempts have been made to include male interests in the books utilized and the topics included for vehicles in the learning-to-read program, these masculine topics are presented in a feminine manner, thus destroying their value to boys. Further complicating the total process of reorienting the program to include boys is the resulting belief that, even after including male topics of interest in the materials of instruction, boys still do less well than girls. It would be normal to assume that girls are more capable than boys. Of course, this is only accurate when it is understood that girls are only more capable in a feminine setting than boys. What would be the comparative status of the two sexes if each were allowed the freedom to function in learning settings adjusted to their own sex? Evidence indicates that sex differences in levels of functioning would disappear.

Changing the learning environment

Providing the needed changes in the learning laboratory to permit the full functioning of both boys and girls requires alteration in the materials used, the techniques of instruction, and change in the staffing patterns of the school. Altering one of these elements of the learning setting without adjustments in the others will not produce the desired changes.

Materials for language instruction

The precise selection of materials for instruction with attention to the needs and interests of the male students must give consideration to the features of adventure, curiosity, and desire for exploration common among boys. These characteristics, and others, should guide the determinations with respect to the materials to be used. The flexibility desired to allow for frequent changes in interests and individuality in the pursuit of studies, dictates a non-textbook approach. A textbook approach to studies is much too restrictive for boys' rapidly changing interests.

Organization of the materials of instruction into centers of interest or learning laboratories which provide collections of books with a single focus, films, pictures, realia, and laboratory materials permitting boys to develop their own study instruments is far more realistic for male students. In fact, such an approach to materials has distinct advantages for girls as well as boys.

Methods of instruction

Knowing that boys function best in circumstances permitting them to learn in individual studies, programs requiring the grouping of students must be viewed as detrimental to the development of boys. Such presentations as are common to the application of the basal reader to reading development, severely handicap male students. Not only do boys find the materials of the basal readers constricting, but the methods of group instruction common to the use of these textbooks is also limiting.

Realizing that each boy tends to function best if he has a large measure of freedom in the associations he develops with other students and in the selection of courses of action he wishes to follow, the method of instruction can be structured accordingly. Learning laboratories can be formed to include the interests of boys, but within these laboratories each boy must be permitted the freedom of personal action which will allow him to utilize his abilities fully. Direction from the teacher must be subtle and through the stimulation of interests and a capitalizing upon expressions of interest by each boy.

Staffing patterns

The balancing of a climate with both feminine and masculine elements indicates a strong need for male teachers. More particularly, there is a need for male primary teachers in the school system. This is not a new concept and in many instances the placement of men in the lower grades would have been accomplished if men were not in such short supply in the elementary programs. The need is well substantiated, however short the supply.

If male teachers cannot be found for employment in programs, it is possible in many school districts to select men as teachers' aides for assignment to the primary classrooms. In such a manner, a male model is provided and the resources are increased for the individualization of methods of instruction.

Assuming limitations upon budgets and the usual restrictions upon numbers of male teachers available to the elementary school program, other approaches to the solution of this problem are possible. Among these alternate solutions would be the use of older, male students as tutors in the primary grades, the utilization of male administrators as frequent assistants to lower-grade teachers, or the use of male resource persons from the community on a regular basis. Any of these devices, used singly or in combination, will support the reorienting of the program along male lines.

Perceptual differences between boys and girls

How a student feels about himself and the manner in which each student catalogs his abilities are seen as vitally important to concepts of adequacy. If the student is satisfied with his attitudes toward himself and can maintain good feelings about himself while functioning in the learning environment, then his chances of succeeding in the school program are substantially enhanced. If a boy cannot retain his maleness in the school setting, it is likely that he will choose not to participate, at least to the real extent of his abilities.

It is suggested in Chapter 2 that learning is essentially the process of shaping and reshaping one's place in new settings. This personal "manufacturing" of perceived placements in the learning environments assumes that each child—each boy—can find himself in the environment. Unfortunately, if the stress is feminine, then many boys will not find themselves able to participate and still retain their concepts of maleness.

Perceived desires

Girls tend to perceive themselves in a social manner which allows for relatively satisfying performance in group situations. These feminine perceptions allow them to focus upon the teacher's function as the director of learning activities without substantial conflict with their perceptions of self. This is not so with boys.

Boys tend to rely upon inner feelings and interpretations of themselves in the light of requirements of the situation. If they cannot remain consistent with their perceptions of maleness as it relates to these feelings, then they will tend not to wish to participate in the learning setting.

Male students develop their feelings toward self largely as a result of societal standards. These standards insist upon a large measure of unique individuality. If the learning environment is functionally group oriented, boys cannot remain true to themselves and participate in the learning process.

Adapting to the learning setting

Whereas girls may adapt easily to the feminine setting of the school, as established by the female teacher model, because of the similarities between this model and the mother figure in the home, boys cannot so easily make such a shift from the father model of the home to the feminine setting of the school. Such adaptations are largely a matter of desire, of course.

For boys to truly desire to make adjustments to the feminine nature of the school, it is necessary for them to give up some traits of maleness and ignore the precepts of self-consistency. It is unfair to expect this of them. Rather, it is the function of the school to permit the continuation of strong feelings of maleness through continued opportunities to function as boys.

Language and personality

Seeing language development as an expression or an extension of personality places the formulation of programs in this field in quite another light. As has been noted, boys have an understandable desire to retain their male character. Therefore, their utilization of male language learning patterns is also understandable.

Male language and cognitive qualities

It is essential that an understanding of the dynamic qualities of language be accepted and that this continuously changing nature of language reflects an extension of each individual's personality. In this manner, educators are able to see language as an expression of thought processes and not as an end in itself.

Thought processes, as expressed through language, are continuous tests of actions and reactions to environmental factors. It is fundamental that the child be able to locate himself in the environment in order that he may participate fully. Feminine climates for learning will, of course, prevent this seeing of oneself in the school setting for many boys. The result is a severe limitation upon language development and growth of the male personality. This also leads to the erroneous assumption that boys are inferior in native abilities relative to growth in language when compared to girls. Acceptance of this appearance of superiority can be dangerous to the formulation of adequate programs of reading and language development for the male half of the student population.

Male and female perceptions of environment

Not only do boys and girls perceive their roles in learning settings as different, but they also have sharply differing perceptions of environments in accord with their sex positions. Boys see their life spaces as having elements not found in the spaces prescribed for girls.

Within the language environments and interest settings for boys are found a number of factors which they perceive as uniquely their own. These include an emphasis upon outdoor life, exploration, sports and games, and particular science orientations. Each of these interests allows vicarious participation of the boy in a male activity.

Girls are less likely to be as restrictive in their perceptions of environmental factors. Nor are they as likely to be able to make sharp distinctions between what they perceive as feminine as opposed to male elements or interests. Because of these less restrictive features of feminine perception, girls are able to function relatively well in nearly any program of reading or language development.

Learning theories and the male

A number of learning theories have been developed to provide guidance for the formulation of effective instructional programs. The more prominent of these theories, the association theories, have a group orientation. This makes these approaches to the learning processes less applicable and less useful in programs providing the freedom required by male students if they are to function well. Unfortunately, the association theories are widely utilized in the methods of the elementary schools. In this manner, boys are again handicapped in the learning setting.

That group of learning theories sometimes identified as field theories emphasizes individual interests and differences. Field theories are based upon nondirective, individually focused approaches to learning. For this reason, field theories are far more applicable to the types of reading and language programs necessary to the development of the potentials of boys.

Effects of individualized learning theories

The application of field theories to the learning environment permits the students to assume more responsibility for individual learning activity. Although the goals of learning programs may be common to boys and girls, each sex—indeed, each student—may pursue the individual activities which seem appropriate to the achievement of these goals.

Boys may utilize such vehicles as adventure, exploration, science, or outdoor interests to develop their potentials in reading or language while girls may utilize such topical centers as music, art, poetry, or family life as the modes for developing abilities in language. Utilizing the field theories methods of instruction, each child can select the vehicles for learning, even choosing to function alternately in essentially feminine or male roles. This method of instruction does not limit the means to achievements of the individual students.

Programs of assessment

Consideration has been given to the importance of including factors in the learning environment which permit boys to function as well as girls. The curriculum, the teachers, and the methodology utilized must allow boys to retain their maleness in each of these aspects of the learning setting. Another factor of equal importance which must be included in the formulation of programs making adequate provisions for boys is the element of appropriate assessment.

Standardized tests

The structuring of uniform tests with a national standardization base is contrary to other considerations which have been given to the adjusting of the school program to make room for boys. The failure of these tests to provide properly for all students results from attempts to make such examinations valid on a universal basis. Theoretically, standardized tests are as appropriate for boys as they are for girls. In fact, these tests have sharp limitations for both sexes.

The use of standardized instruments of assessment fails to consider the unique interests and methods of participation of boys as opposed to girls. Moreover, these instruments assume a common standard for instruction at given levels in the school program and with respect to elements in the program. If the learning theory being used in the classroom is one which provides for individual learning patterns, then the commonness essential to the formulation of standardized instruments does not exist. In such a case, the standardized test becomes a program handicap rather than a support item.

Comparative methods of assessment

Utilization of methods of assessment that are established upon a uniform standard applicable to all students is directly contrary to a concern for individuality in program development.

The degrees to which each student is free to develop language abilities and able to assess achievements in this field are dependent upon individual methods of assessment. Each technique for assessment must be applied to the goals and activities of the single student. Only in this manner is it possible to measure actual growth of the individual and relate the content of the measurement devices to the actual program of learning.

Boys must be able to assess their own achievements through the application of devices for assessment which are directly related to their own programs of learning, and these learning programs must be fully consistent with their primary interests and with the male modes of functioning.

To avoid the traditional pitfalls of program development which discriminate against male students, the schools and the programs of instruction developed to complete the learning environment must be sufficiently flexible to allow focus upon the factors of individuality in a manner which encourages learning for all children. This is not only sound educationally, but such freedom is consistent with the tenets of our national way of life.

Index